EVALUATING THE CAPACITY OF THE VA TO CARE FOR VETERAN PATIENTS

HEARING

BEFORE THE

OF THE

COMMITTEE ON VETERANS' AFFAIRS
U.S. HOUSE OF REPRESENTATIVES

ONE HUNDRED THIRTEENTH CONGRESS

SECOND SESSION

Monday June 23, 2014

Serial No. 113–76

Printed for the use of the Committee on Veterans' Affairs

Available via the World Wide Web: http://www.fdsys.gov
http://www.house.gov/reform

U.S. GOVERNMENT PRINTING OFFICE

WASHINGTON : 2014

89–375 PDF

For sale by the Superintendent of Documents, U.S. Government Printing Office
Internet: bookstore.gpo.gov   Phone: toll free (866) 512–1800; DC area (202) 512–1800
Fax: (202) 512–2104   Mail: Stop IDCC, Washington, DC 20402–0001

COMMITTEE ON VETERANS' AFFAIRS

JEFF MILLER, *Chairman*

DOUG LAMBORN, Colorado
GUS M. BILIRAKIS, Florida *Vice-Chairman*
DAVID P. ROE, Tennessee
BILL FLORES, Texas
JEFF DENHAM, California
JON RUNYAN, New Jersey
DAN BENISHEK, Michigan
TIM HUELSKAMP, Kansas
MIKE COFFMAN, Colorado
BRAD R. WENSTRUP, Ohio
PAUL COOK, California
JACKIE WALORSKI, Indiana
DAVID JOLLY, Florida

MICHAEL H. MICHAUD, Maine, *Ranking Member*
CORRINE BROWN, Florida
MARK TAKANO, California
JULIA BROWNLEY, California
DINA TITUS, Nevada
ANN KIRKPATRICK, Arizona
RAUL RUIZ, California
GLORIA NEGRETE MCLEOD, California
ANN M. KUSTER, New Hampshire
BETO O' ROURKE, Texas
TIMOTHY J. WALZ, Minnesota

Jon Towers, *Staff Director*
Nancy Dolan, *Democratic Staff Director*

Pursuant to clause 2(e)(4) of Rule XI of the Rules of the House, public hearing records of the Committee on Veterans' Affairs are also published in electronic form. **The printed hearing record remains the official version.** Because electronic submissions are used to prepare both printed and electronic versions of the hearing record, the process of converting between various electronic formats may introduce unintentional errors or omissions. Such occurrences are inherent in the current publication process and should diminish as the process is further refined.

CONTENTS

EVALUATING THE CAPACITY OF THE VA TO CARE FOR VETERAN PATIENTS

Monday, June 23, 2014

U.S. HOUSE OF REPRESENTATIVES
COMMITTEE ON VETERANS' AFFAIRS
WASHINGTON, D.C.

OPENING STATEMENT OF CHAIRMAN JEFF MILLER

The committee met, pursuant to notice, at 7:30 p.m., in Room 334, Cannon House Office Building, Hon. Jeff Miller [chairman of the committee] presiding.

Present: Representatives Miller, Lamborn, Bilirakis, Roe, Flores, Benishek, Huelskamp, Coffman, Wenstrup, Walorski, Jolly, Michaud, Takano, Brownley, Titus, Kirkpatrick, Ruiz, Negrete McLeod, Kuster, O'Rourke, and Walz.

The CHAIRMAN. Good evening. The committee will come to order.

Welcome to tonight's full committee oversight hearing evaluating the capacity of the VA to care for veteran patients. During our proceedings this evening, we hopefully will assess the Department of Veterans Affairs efforts to increase the capacity and efficiency of medical facility operations and ultimately to improve access to care for veteran patients who have been facing unacceptably long wait times at VA facilities across the country.

Important to those efforts is the status of VA's Accelerating Access to Care Initiative. The initiative was launched in late May in response to the Department's current wait time crisis, and information released last Thursday suggests that it, in coordination with VA's other efforts, has led to the scheduling of approximately 200,000 appointments from May 15th to June 1st.

I am glad to see the Department seems to be taking its access failure seriously and is taking steps accordingly to improve the timeliness of care for veteran patients; however, I do have serious concerns about VA's efforts to date. One of my concerns is the continued lack of detailed information that Congress has received about the initiative, making this yet another in a long and continually increasing list of examples of VA failing to act in an open and transparent manner.

The committee requested a briefing from the Department on the Accelerating Access to Care Initiative on June the 2nd. I followed up this request with a formal letter to Acting Secretary Gibson on June 5th, requesting an immediate briefing on the initiative. It has now been 19 days since that request for an immediate briefing, and no further information or acknowledgement of our request has been received. It baffles me as to why the Department failed to provide this committee with the information we requested on a program of this size and this importance. If VA's work has indeed led to 200,000 more appointments for veteran patients so far, what is there to hide?

More importantly, over the last several weeks, investigations by the Inspector General's office and the Department itself have proven that the VA healthcare system suffers from a systemic lack of integrity. Data manipulation and patient waiting times were found to be widespread, and given that, how can Congress, the American taxpayer and our Nation's veterans and their families have any confidence in these latest numbers that the Department has released? Furthermore, if there were actions that VA could have taken to increase access to care for veteran patients, why were those actions not taken long before now?

As part of the Accelerating Access to Care Initiative, VA claims to be taking steps to, in the Department's own words, systematically review clinical capacity, ensure primary care clinic panels are correctly sized and achieving the desired level of productivity, extend or flex clinic hours on nights and weekends, increase the use of care in the community, and reach out to veterans to coordinate the acceleration of their care.

Each of these actions should have been operational components of regular VA business long before now, and VA has had the statutory authority to use these options previously.

We know that at least 35 veterans in the Phoenix area alone died while waiting to receive VA care, though I suspect that number may rise in the coming weeks and months. We know that 57,000 veterans nationwide have been waiting 90 days or more for their first VA appointment and we know that 64,000 veterans who were enrolled in the system over the last decade never received the appointment that they requested. It is too late for those 35 Phoenix area veterans and it may be too late for other veterans who have been waiting for weeks, months and in some cases years.

So I ask again, if there were actions that VA could have taken to increase access to care for veteran patients, why were those actions not taken long before now?

PREPARED STATEMENT OF JEFF MILLER, Chairman

Good evening. The Committee will come to order.

Welcome to today's Full Committee oversight hearing, "Evaluating the Capacity of the VA to care for Veteran Patients."

During tonight's proceedings, we will assess the Department of Veterans Affairs' (VA's) efforts to increase the capacity and efficiency of medical facility operations and, ultimately, improve access to care for veteran patients who have been facing unacceptably long wait times at VA facilities across the country. Important to those efforts is the status of VA's Accelerating Access to Care Initiative.

The Initiative was launched in late May in response to the Department's current wait time crisis and information released last Thursday suggest that it – in coordination with VA's other efforts

- has led to approximately two-hundred thousand increased appointments from May 15th to June 1st.

I am glad to see that the Department seems to be taking its access failures seriously and is taking steps accordingly to improve the timeliness of care for veteran patients. However, I do have serious concerns about VA's efforts to-date. One of my concerns is the lack of detailed information Congress has received about the Initiative, making this yet another in a long and continually increasing list of examples of VA failing to act in an open and transparent manner.

The Committee requested a briefing from the Department on the Accelerating Access to Care Initiative on June 2nd. I followed-up this request with a formal letter to Acting Secretary Gibson on June 5th requesting an immediate briefing on the Initiative. It has now been nineteen days since that request for an immediate briefing and no further information or acknowledgment of my request has been received. It baffles me as to why the Department failed to provide this Committee with the information we requested on a program of this size and importance. If VA's work has indeed led to two-hundred thousand more appointments for veteran patients so far, what is there to hide?

More importantly, over the last several weeks, investigations by the VA Inspector General and the Department itself have proven that the VA health care system suffers from a systemic lack of integrity. Data manipulation of patient waiting times was found to be widespread. Given that, how can Congress, the American taxpayer, and our nation's veterans and their families have any confidence in these latest numbers the Department has released?

Furthermore, if there were actions that VA could have taking to increase access to care for veterans patients, why were those actions not taken long before now? As part of the Accelerating Access to Care Initiative, VA claims to be taking steps to, in the Department's own words, -

- "systematically [review] clinical capacity;"
- "[ensure] primary care clinic panels are correctly sized and achieving the desired level of productivity;"
- "[extend or flex] clinic hours on nights and weekends;"
- "[increase] the use of care in the community;" and,
- "[reach] out to veterans to coordinate the acceleration of their care."

Each of these actions should have been operational components of regular VA business long before now and VA had statutory authority to use these options previously. We know that at least thirty-five veterans in the Phoenix-area alone died while waiting to receive VA care – though I suspect that number may rise in the coming weeks and months.

We know that fifty-seven thousand veterans nationwide have been waiting ninety days or more for their first VA appointment. And, we know that sixty-four thousand veterans who enrolled in the VA healthcare system over the last decade never received the appointment they requested. It is too late for those thirty-five Phoenix area veterans and it may be too late for other veterans who have been waiting for weeks, months, and – in some cases – years.

So I ask again, if there were actions that VA could have taking to increase access to care for veterans patients, why were those actions not taken long before now? With that, I now yield to Ranking Member Michaud for any opening statement he may have.

With that, I yield to the ranking member, Mr. Michaud, for his opening statement.

OPENING STATEMENT OF MIKE MICHAUD, RANKING MEMBER

Mr. Michaud. Thank you very much, Mr. Chairman, for once again having this hearing tonight.

Providing timely, quality, safe care to veterans is the primary mission of the Department of Veterans Affairs. Integral to accomplishing this mission is the ability to successfully measure the capacity and capability of the organization.

Mr. Chairman, at this point in time, I do not have much confidence that VA has been able to do that analysis. I firmly believe that if you do not have good numbers on which to base calculations, then you cannot possibly begin to accurately measure the capacity or demand. Anticipating capacity and demand is central to good strategic planning. Clearly, VA is struggling to get a handle on how many veterans are undergoing or waiting for treatment. It seems to me having a significant number of patients on the waiting list indicates a system that is overwhelmed and unprepared. VHA simply cannot handle the increasing number of veterans to whom we have a moral obligation to provide sound treatment.

The VA OIG reported in testimony on March 2013 that VHA Office of Productivity, Efficiency and Staffing conducted studies in 2006 of 14 specialty care services. The report had nine recommendations. One of the recommendations was to have the VHA develop relative value unit productivity standards and staffing guidance for the field. I recognize this is a complex process and VA healthcare has continued to change over the years, but 8 years to develop this system is too long and is unacceptable.

While Dr. Lynch states in testimony that by the end of September 2014, all VHA physicians will have productivity standards in place, I am skeptical of the usefulness of those standards, due to the current crisis.

Today, I would like to hear from VA how they are measuring capacity and a timeline for when this will be done, and most importantly, any additional resources that may be needed to ensure VA is fully fulfilling the primary mission of providing healthcare to our Nation's veterans.

Mr. Chairman, I know that the vast majority of the Department employees are hardworking and dedicated to caring for our veterans, for that I applaud them, but we still have a responsibility and duty to take care of all of our veterans.

And I look forward to hearing from the VA tonight, and I want to thank you for coming this evening. With that, I yield back.

PREPARED STATEMENT OF MIKE MICHAUD, Ranking Member

* Thank you Mr. Chairman.
* Providing timely, quality, safe care to veterans is the primary mission of the Department of Veterans Affairs.

* Integral to accomplishing this mission is the ability to successfully measure the capacity and capabilities of the organization.

* Mr. Chairman, at this point in time, I do not have much confidence VA has been able to do that analysis.

* I firmly believe if you do not have good numbers on which to base calculations, then you cannot possibly begin to accurately measure capacity or demand.

* Anticipating capacity and demand is central to good strategic planning.

* Clearly VA is struggling to get a handle on how many veterans are undergoing or waiting for treatment. It seems to me having a significant number of patients on waiting lists indicates a system that is overwhelmed and unprepared. VHA simply cannot handle the increasing number of veterans to whom we have a moral obligation to provide sound treatment.

* The VA OIG reported in testimony on March 2013, that VHA's Office of Productivity, Efficiency, and Staffing conducted studies in 2006 of 14 specialty care services. The report had nine recommendations. One of the recommendations was to have VHA develop Relative Value Unit productivity standards and staffing guidance for the field.

* I recognize this is a complicated process and VA health care has continued to change over the years, but eight years to develop this system is too long. It's unacceptable.

* While Dr. Lynch states in testimony that by the end of September 2014, all VHA physicians will have productivity standards in place, I am skeptical of the usefulness of those standards due to the current crisis.

* Today, I would like to hear from VA how they are measuring capacity, a timeline for when they will be done, and most importantly, any additional resources that may be needed to ensure VA is fulfilling the primary mission of providing health care to the nation's veterans.

* Mr. Chairman, I know that the vast majority of the Department's employees are hard-working and dedicated to caring for veterans. For that, I applaud them.

* I look forward to hearing from the VA today and thank them for coming.

The CHAIRMAN. Thank you very much, Mr. Michaud.

We are honored to be joined this evening by Dr. Thomas Lynch, the Assistant Deputy Under Secretary for Health for Clinical Operation's, and he is accompanied by Dr. Carolyn Clancy, the Assistant Deputy Under Secretary for Health for Quality, Safety and Value.

We appreciate you both for being here tonight, and Dr. Lynch, we appreciate you coming for your return engagement to an evening function.

You are recognized for your opening statement.

OPENING STATEMENT OF DR. LYNCH

Dr. Lynch. Good evening, Chairman Miller, Ranking Member Michaud and members of the committee.

Thank you for the opportunity to discuss the provision of timely, accessible and quality care for veterans. I am accompanied today by Dr. Carolyn Clancy, Assistant Deputy Under Secretary for Health, for Quality, Safety and Value.

At the outset, let me address the significant issue that has been the focus of the committee, the VA and the American public: that is, the issue of wait times. No veteran should ever have to wait an unreasonable amount of time to receive the care that they have earned through their service and their sacrifice. America's veterans should know they will receive the highest quality healthcare from VA. While we realize the timeliness of these services is in question, VA acknowledges and is committed to correcting the unacceptable practices in patient scheduling. As my colleague, Philip Matkovsky, stated on June 9th, this is a breach of trust. It is irresponsible, it is indefensible and it is unacceptable.

I also apologize, as he did, to our veterans, their families and loved ones, members of Congress, the Veterans Service Organization, our employees, and the American people. These practices are not consistent with our values as a Department, and we are working to fix the problem.

VA has a physician workforce of more than 25,000 physicians representing over 30 specialties. VA now has comprehensive information about the staffing levels at each medical center, as well as the productivity of our physician workforce, utilizing a standard healthcare measure of relative value units, or RVUs. RVUs consider the time and the intensity of medical services delivered.

Optimizing physician productivity is critical to our ability to determine clinical capacity and mobilize our clinical assets to rapidly address unacceptable delays in service.

Supporting a productive workforce requires appropriate support staff ratios as well as the necessary capital infrastructure to ensure that the clinics run as efficiently as possible. The difference between the estimated capacity and our current workload represents the amount of additional care we could provide to address veterans waiting for care. VA has accelerated the adoption of productivity standards because they are critical in determining VHA's capacity and improving timely access to quality care for veterans.

We are about a year ahead of schedule in completing action plans based on the recommendations of the OIG in late 2012. We will have productivity standards in place for all physicians in VHA by the end of this fiscal year.

Like all of healthcare, VA has transitioned to a system in which outpatient care is increasingly important, especially for the management of chronic conditions. VA has established the Nation's largest medical home approach to primary care, in which people receive care from teams, and in addition, to face-to-face visits, they receive advice and consultation, which can be provided through technology, through telephone calls, secure emails and tele-health.

Leveraging these capabilities to deliver veteran-centric care requires investments in education, training, and the ongoing evaluation to assure that services are focused on the needs and preferences of individual veterans. Since the majority of U.S. physicians receive some training in a VA facility, we have also invested in contemporary approaches to undergraduate and graduate training that reinforce the importance of teamwork and technological skills, and leverage research investments to assure that the promise of these new models achieves the goal of personalized veteran-centric care.

Mr. Chairman, the health and well-being of the men and women who have bravely and selflessly served this Nation remains VA's highest priority. The work continues, and we will not be finished until VA can assess capacity, productivity and staffing standards for all specialties, and provide ready access to high quality, efficient care available to our Nation's veterans. We must regain the trust of the veterans we serve. VA leadership and our dedicated workforce are fully engaged.

This concludes my testimony. My colleague and I are prepared to answer any questions you and the other members of the committee may have.

PREPARED STATEMENT OF THE HON. CORRINE BROWN

Thank you, Chairman Miller and Ranking Member Michaud for calling this hearing tonight.

My many years of serving on this committee and meetings with veterans have opened my eyes to the many services the VA provides for our veterans.

One issue that I was recently exposed to was tele-health and tele-medicine. I was prepared to dislike remote controlled health care. How could a veteran receive care in his home? But I was pleasantly surprised to find out the care was equivalent to going to the VA clinic, but not having to travel all that way.

And the veteran loved it! VA medical staff reviewed the information and advised the veteran on what actions to take. Emergency personnel would be called if that was deemed necessary. I thank Mr. Michaud for making tele-health a priority for the VA.

This brings me to my main point. Veterans love VA care. However, there is not enough VA to go around. As the recent experiences of VA hospitals being built show, including in my Orlando, building a hospital is not the VA's strong point.

The VA operates 1,700 sites of care, and conducts approximately 85 million appointments each year, which comes to 236,000 health care appointments each day.

The latest American Customer Satisfaction Index, an independent customer service survey, ranks VA customer satisfaction among Veteran patients among the best in the nation and equal to or better than ratings for private sector hospitals.

It is not necessary to get veterans to a VA facility to get VA quality care. The VA is an admitted leader in treating the issues veterans suffer from: TBI, PTSD, prosthetics and Agent Orange maladies.

If we bring community organizations into VA care, veterans could get care where they live. Allowing private practice doctors to treat veterans would not be fair to the veteran or the doctor. If there is no follow up on the care, who is responsible? However, if community non-profit health providers are contracted with the VA, that follow up can be tracked. In addition, the VA could open an office or a wing in the community facility which would bring VA care to the veteran also.

I look forward to hearing from the witness on this issue.

PREPARED STATEMENT OF HON. GLORIA NEGRETE MCLEOD

Thank you, Mr. Chairmen. There are serious problems at the VA that must be resolved so veterans can be treated in a timely manner. VA must work diligently to implement new metrics that accurately show how many doctors and hospitals it needs to care for our growing veteran population. VA doctors must be willing to embrace best practices from the private sector. The belief that VA is a unique public health system does not excuse inefficiency.

Private sector care can complement but cannot replace health care at the VA. It is my hope that the current crisis in providing health care will compel all VA employees to think outside the box on how to improve care for our veterans.

That also means that Congress must work with VA as a partner and not just as a critic. It is right for Congress to hold VA accountable for the harm caused toward veteran patients. Yet holding hearings without working on solutions does not help veterans find timely care.

I look forward to working with VA to move through this crisis and will continue to support the Inspector General and Department of Justice's efforts to investigate and prosecute those who have committed malpractice.

STATEMENT OF DR. LYNCH

The CHAIRMAN. Thank you very much, Dr. Lynch.

How quickly can VA hire clinical staff under current authorities?

Dr. Lynch. Mr. Chairman, I don't have the answer to that question. I know that our current processes, particularly in human resources, are slow. We are putting processes in place to speed those processes, to speed that process so that we can hire physicians more efficiently and more quickly.

The CHAIRMAN. Are there any impediments that we as a legislative body can do to assist in removing some of the barriers?

Dr. Lynch. At the moment, Mr. Chairman, I can't think of any.

Dr. Clancy. I would simply add that -- sorry. Sorry about that.

I would just add that some part of the reason it takes a bit of time is the credentialing and privileging process, which I think you would want us all to be rigorous about. We are investigating ways to try to speed that up, but the human resources part is part one.

The CHAIRMAN. What is the expected cost of the Accelerating Access to Care Initiative and how are you funding it currently?

Dr. Lynch. Right now the expected cost that we have invested is approximately $312 million. It is being funded based on monies that we have been able to recover from across VHA.

The CHAIRMAN. Can you tell me if any additional authorities have been granted to VA medical centers as a result of the initiative?

Dr. Lynch. What do you mean by additional authorities?

The CHAIRMAN. Any authorities being granted to help speed the process along.

Dr. Lynch. Other than asking the facilities to look at their processes and the efficiency of their processes, see if they can identify internal capacity, and if they cannot, to let us know what resources they need to provide that care in the community. That process has occurred. The facilities have made their requests, and to date, we have distributed approximately $312 million, of which approximately $152 million have been obligated at this point.

The CHAIRMAN. Dr. Lynch, according to the Physician's Foundation 2012 survey of America's physicians, over 80 percent of the primary care physicians in the United States see between 11 and 61 patients per day, and U.S. physicians in general see an average of over 20 patients per day. Can you tell us what the average daily patient load of a VA primary care physician is?

Dr. Lynch. Right now the average patient load is approximately 10 patients per day. If I could qualify that by saying that I think we need to assure that we understand what support staff our physicians have and what capacity they have in the way of rooms to facilitate their ability to see patients. I think it is not just the physician's ability and willingness to see patients, it is also the support that we provide them and it is the rooms that we give them so they can see patients in an efficient fashion.

The CHAIRMAN. But you --

Dr. Lynch. The range, by the way, is from 6 per day up to about 22 per day for our physicians.

The CHAIRMAN. But you are the agency that designs the clinics, designs the hospitals, designs the facilities, so you would know how many rooms would be needed, I would suspect, in order for patients to be seen.

Dr. Lynch. Congressman, many of our facilities are 50 or 60 years old and were designed in an era when outpatient healthcare was not the predominant mode of healthcare delivery. VA in the mid 1990s converted from an inpatient model to an outpatient model. We are still challenged by facilities that were not constructed for the outpatient model of care.

The CHAIRMAN. So if I went to a new facility, I should suspect that the doctors there will be seeing more patients than those in the older facilities?

Dr. Lynch. The VA has been working to put in place templates that facilitate the delivery of care using the medical home model, so that we are redesigning new clinics in our outpatient facilities to optimize the ability of our physicians to provide care and to see patients in that model, yes, congresswoman -- Congressman.

The CHAIRMAN. One other question, if you would. The Office of Special Counsel wrote a letter to the president today.

Dr. Lynch. Yes.

The CHAIRMAN. The OSC cites the case of a veteran with a 100-percent service-connected psychiatric condition that resided in a Brockton, Massachusetts, medical health facility for 8 years. Are you familiar with that particular incident?

Dr. Lynch. Yes, sir.

The CHAIRMAN. And in those 8 years at the facility, this veteran apparently had only one psychiatric note in his chart. Is that true?

Dr. Lynch. That is true, sir.

The CHAIRMAN. One note in 8 years.

Dr. Lynch. That is unacceptable, sir.

The CHAIRMAN. Despite the fact that the Office of the Medical Inspector substantiated that this occurred, it also stated in the same letter, it had no impact on that patient's care. Can you believe that?

Dr. Lynch. Congressman, the Office of the Medical Inspector is unique in healthcare. We don't see it in the private sector. It is VA's arm to evaluate objectively outside of the facility concerns about the quality of care.

I understand that the Office of Special Counsel has raised concerns. VA and our Acting Secretary have taken those concerns very seriously. We need to take them seriously, because VA is in a position where we have to reestablish our integrity.

He has established a group, a commission, who will evaluate those concerns. The report is due in 14 days. I think it is important we understand what that review shows before we draw any conclusions.

The CHAIRMAN. Thank you.

Mr. Michaud, you are recognized.

Mr. Michaud. Thank you very much, Mr. Chairman.

Once again, thank you Dr. Lynch and Dr. Clancy for coming here this evening.

We understand that the Accelerated Access to Care Initiative is designed to ensure access to care by enhancing resources within VA facilities and also sending veterans promptly to community-based care and non-VA care when needed care is not readily available at the VA facility.

What is the role of PC-3's in VA Accelerating Access to Care Initiative?

Dr. Lynch. PC3 as it develops will be another model that we can use to provide care in the community. PC3 is just in the process of being stood up. Some sites have greater availability of PC3 services than others. It is, however, an option that we can use to identify community providers who are willing to provide care and to meet certain conditions of the contract which specify that care will be provided within 30 days, that we will receive reports in a timely fashion.

So PC3 is an enhanced method of providing care in the community that gives benefit to the VA, because it assures timeliness and assures that we get records back in a timely fashion.

Dr. Clancy. I would also just add that they assure some minimal level of quality, I mean, foundational level of quality in terms of contracting with hospitals that are accredited by the joint commission or a relevant accreditor, that the plans that they are contracting with have met standards for the National Committee on Quality Assurance and so forth, and we are going to be working with them to figure out how do we even make those standards a bit higher.

Mr. Michaud. Thank you. The committee is aware that the VA had conducted several pilot projects, such as Project HERO and Project ARCH before implementing PC3. VA also has indicated that in designing PC3, it used lessons learned from these pilot programs to develop a solution which is coordinated, convenient and consistent with VA quality standards.

My question, then, is now that PC3 is up and running across the country, are all VA medical centers using this program as part of the solution?

Dr. Lynch. I believe the answer, Congressman, is when it is available and when the services are available, it is being used, yes.

Mr. Michaud. So it is not throughout all of VA medical centers, then?

Dr. Lynch. In certain areas, the contractors are having to identify providers and are standing up their services. In other areas, services are available and PC3 is being used, to the best of my knowledge.

Mr. Michaud. Okay. We understand that PC3 is not a mandatory program. How can we have a VA medical center fully utilizing PC3 and utilizing the potential of this program if it is not a mandatory program?

Dr. Lynch. It would be my hope, understanding the benefits of the PC3 process, that it would be advantageous to the medical centers to use that program. As I mentioned, there are standards for timeliness of providing services and there are standards for the receipt of work product after the services have been provided.

Mr. Michaud. Okay. How does the VA distinguish between short-term and long-term capacity shortfalls and how does the VA respond different to the long-term and short-term shortfalls?

Dr. Lynch. I think as our data becomes more reliable and as we see increasing use of the electronic wait list, which has now been mandated, we will have the option to see our demand handled in one of two ways: either as a completed appointment or as a patient who ends up on the electronic wait list. Depending upon whether this is a short-term increase in the requirement for services, in which case the VA may find it very convenient to buy that in the community, there was also the possibility that this is part of a longer term trend, in which case, the VA may want to consider how much is it going to cost me to buy this and ultimately do we need to make a decision that it will be more cost-effective for us to identify the providers and make the service in-house.

So I think short term, PC3, non-VA care provides the opportunity for us to offer prompt services to veterans when we don't have the capacity. In the long-term, when we see trends, it gives us the option of making decisions about whether we should continue to buy this in the community, because of its complexity, or whether we think we can offer it in-house.

Mr. Michaud. Thank you, Mr. Chairman.

The CHAIRMAN. Mr. Lamborn, you are recognized for 5 minutes.

Mr. Lamborn. Thank you, Mr. Chairman.

Dr. Lynch, in the last 2 weeks, the number of veterans in my district in Colorado Springs that contacted my office asking for help while trying to see a doctor has more than doubled. One veteran described how he was referred to get a biopsy done on his thyroid to determine whether or not he had cancer only to be told he couldn't be seen for 2 months. I can't imagine having to wait for 2 months to even just get a test done when you have a possible cancerous growth.

Tell me what options, please, are available to the Denver VA Medical Center to expedite a biopsy appointment in particular, especially based on medical necessity and if there is the possibility of a life-threatening condition?

Dr. Lynch. Congressman, based on what you are telling me, if services cannot be provided in less than 30 days, that is an unacceptable waiting time, and the Denver VA facility should be able to identify a community provider to offer those services.

Mr. Lamborn. Okay. That would be the fee basis approach that we have talked about?

Dr. Lynch. That would be the use of non-VA care or the fee basis approach, yes.

Mr. Lamborn. Okay, so 55 days for that type of procedure is unacceptable, you would agree?

Dr. Lynch. That would certainly be my impression, Congressman.

Mr. Lamborn. All right. Thank you. Now, the data included in the VA's bi-monthly access data update makes me worry that this problem might be getting worse before it gets better, especially in Colorado. And myself and Representative Mike Coffman have a lot of these same concerns.

Although the report shows the number of veterans on the electronic wait list across the country dropping slightly, the electronic wait list at the Denver VA Medical Center, where many of my constituents receive care, doubled in the last 15 days. It went from 1,632 to 3,331. What could have caused that number to double in 15 days when around the country, it was dropping slightly?

Dr. Lynch. I don't have the specifics on Denver, Congressman. I will be happy to try and get that information for you.

I can tell you that at the moment, the electronic wait list is going to be dynamic. There are two processes that are occurring. We are working down the near list, the new enrollee appointment request. Those patients are either being given scheduled appointments or they are being put on the electronic wait list.

So it is possible that some of the patients that were on the near list have been moved to the electronic wait list, but exactly, you know, why they are accumulating on the electronic wait list, I don't know, but I think we have the capacity to find that out.

Mr. Lamborn. Okay. Well, if you could get back to me on that, I would appreciate it.

Dr. Lynch. I will do that, Congressman.

PREPARED STATEMENT OF THOMAS LYNCH, M.D.

Good morning, Chairman Miller, Ranking Member Michaud, and Members of the Committee. Thank you for the opportunity to discuss the capacity and demand for services in VHA. I am accompanied today by Carolyn Clancy, M.D., Assistant Deputy Under Secretary for Health for Quality, Safety and Value.

At the outset, let me address the significant issue that has been the focus of this Committee, VA, and the American public the last many weeks. That is the issue of wait times. No Veteran should ever have to wait an unreasonable amount of time to receive the care they have earned through their service and sacrifice.

America's Veterans should know they will receive the highest quality health care in a timely manner from VA. Last year, we scheduled 85 million outpatient visits and acted upon 25 million consults for specialized services. While we realize that the timeliness of these services is in question, VA acknowledges and is committed to correcting unacceptable practices in patient scheduling. These practices are not consistent with our values as a Department, and we are working to fix the problems.

VHA has a physician workforce of more than 18,000 full time equivalents (FTEs) representing over 30 specialties. The largest components of the physician workforce include our Internal Medicine (largely primary care) physicians and psychiatrists. VHA maintains a comprehensive database of the physician workforce that provides information about the staffing levels for each Medical Center and calculates the productivity of our physician workforce utilizing a standard health care measure of relative value units (RVU) per physician clinical FTE. RVUs consider the time and the intensity of the medical services delivered and have been utilized by Medicare since the early 1990's. VHA is currently using this database to establish productivity standards and to assess the capacity of our provider workforce. For our primary care physicians there are clear panel size expectations that define the number of active patients assigned to each primary care provider. Panel sizes vary depending on a number of factors. The current average panel size is 1,194, but panels may be adjusted up or down depending on levels of support staff, space (exam rooms) and patient complexity. VHA is assessing the current demand for services in relation to primary care panel capacity as well as the productivity of the primary care providers and all physicians and associate providers at each of our medical centers.

During a February 2014 hearing before the Subcommittee on Health, we reported VHA's progress in implementing an industry-accepted RVU-based approach for assessing productivity and efficiency for specialty care physicians. More recently, on May 1, 2014, VHA briefed the physicians on the Subcommittee on the RVU-based productivity and staffing work. Although our focus on establishing an RVU-based model to assess specialty physician productivity did not initially include Internal Medicine/Primary Care, the foundation we put in place for specialty care is now being leveraged to assess productivity, efficiency, staffing and capacity within our primary care services. Ready access to care is our highest priority and we are mobilizing our workforce accordingly.

VHA delivers care that encompasses nearly three dozen different specialties in a variety of settings, and access to care varies across those specialties and settings. Our large acute care academic facilities generally employ the full complement of specialty physicians and have the capability to provide comprehensive services while our smaller or rural facilities may be challenged to recruit and retain specialty physicians. Aligning the current demand with our ability to provide these services is part of our active work.

Optimizing physician productivity is critical to our ability to determine clinical capacity and mobilize our clinical assets to rapidly address unacceptable delays in services to our Veterans. Supporting a productive workforce requires appropriate support staff ratios as well as the necessary capital infrastructure, e.g., exam room capacity, to ensure that the clinics run as efficiently as possible. The key elements of capacity include: (1) the supply of clinical providers (physicians, psychologists, optometrists, podiatrists, and associate providers such as nurse practitioners and physician assistants) within VHA; (2) the amount of services that each of these providers can safely deliver (productivity); and (3) a modern information technology infrastructure that supports and enhances clinical information for the patient and providers. We currently know the supply of our provider workforce and, assuming a productivity expectation, we can estimate what our capacity could be. The difference between this estimated capacity and our current workload represents the amount of additional care we could potentially absorb to address Veterans waiting for care.

Productivity expectations are critical in determining VHA's capacity and, VHA has accelerated the adoption of productivity standards for all physicians, modeled on an industry-accepted RVU-based approach. By the end of June 2014, VHA will have standards in place to measure productivity and efficiency for 29 different specialties, representing 91 percent of VHA's physicians, psychologists, optometrists, podiatrists, and chiropractors. All VHA physicians will have productivity standards in place by the end of September 2014.

The same results-oriented approach we have taken to implement physician productivity and staffing standards will be applied to address today's challenge to measure and maximize our clinical capacity. The work continues, and we will not be finished until VHA can assess capacity, productivity, and staffing standards for all specialties, and provide ready access to high quality, efficient care to our Nation's Veterans.

To fulfill VHA's primary mission of providing patient care and to assist in providing an adequate supply of health personnel to the Nation, VA is authorized by Title 38 Section 7302 to provide clinical education and training programs for developing health professionals. VA conducts the largest education and training effort for health professionals in the U.S. This provides VA with a unique opportunity to recruit these medical professionals, already familiar with the VA health care system.

VA recognizes that rural communities face challenges in ensuring access to health care providers. VA is working to develop an effective rural workforce strategy to recruit locally for a broad range of health-related professions. These strategies include training, technology, collaboration, and academic affiliations. Empowering Veteran patients with telehealth technology and targeted health communications have proven to be an important way to provide quality care in the daily lives of Veterans.

In addition, VA collaborates with Federal partners such as the Department of Health and Human Services to establish pilot projects with community-based providers; the Department of Defense to improve access to care for Service members and Veterans through sharing agreements; and the Department of Housing and Urban Development (HUD) to coordinate the HUD–VA Supportive Housing program.

Conclusion

Mr. Chairman, the health and well-being of the men and women who have bravely and selflessly served this Nation remains VA's highest priority. We must regain the trust of Veterans we serve one Veteran at a time, and VA leaders and our dedicated workforce, over a third of who are Veterans themselves, are fully engaged. This concludes my testimony. My colleague and I are prepared to answer any questions you or the other Members of the Committee may have.

Mr. Lamborn. Okay. Thank you.

Now, you stated in your written statement that the average current number of patients assigned to each primary care provider is 1,194. How does that compare with the private sector?

Dr. Lynch. The private sector medical home model can vary, with panels of anywhere from 1,000 up to about 2,000. It depends on the complexity of those patients, it depends on the resources available and the support for the physicians seeing those patients. VA patients are often older. Patients in the private sector may be younger, healthier and may not require the intensity of care that VA patients require.

Dr. Clancy, would you have any comment?

Dr. Clancy. No. Sorry. I would agree with all of that. We also -- the VA's medical home in the primary care setting is also unique for being integrated in many of our facilities with mental health providers who are right there if those needs arise.

Mr. Lamborn. Okay. Thank you. One last question I want to get in. You note in your written testimony that the VA is adopting productivity standards that are modeled on industry-accepted standards. I am really glad to hear that, but what has been the case, what has been the standard up until now?

Dr. Lynch. Sadly, Congressman, there hasn't been a standard to this point. We are now using the relative value unit to evaluate the productivity of our providers. We are then using that information to determine, number one, are they meeting minimum productivity standards, number two, if they are not, why not.

It could be a matter of support and available resources. It could be a matter that there are not enough patients for them to see, and in that case, either we need to identify more patients or we need to figure out a way that we can move their capacity to another facility, perhaps using something like tele-health.

Mr. Lamborn. Thank you.

The CHAIRMAN. Ms. Negrete McLeod, you are recognized for 5 minutes.

Ms. Negrete McLeod. I really have no questions. I yield back.

The CHAIRMAN. Mr. Takano, you are recognized for 5 minutes.

Mr. Takano. Thank you, Mr. Chairman.

And thank you, Dr. Lynch and Dr. Clancy, for appearing before us today.

I understand that from 2008 to 2013, non-VA care outpatient visits grew from 8.9 million, or 9 million, to 15.3 million, a 72 percent increase. Do we have any way of knowing about the comparison between non-VA care versus in-house care, its efficacy and its costs?

Dr. Lynch. I don't have the comparative data from those years. I can tell you in the last fiscal year, we spent approximately $4.8 billion on non-VA care, but I would have to try and get previous data to see how our use of non-VA care has increased or has changed as we have seen increasing outpatient requirements.

Mr. Takano. It seems to me that if we want to expand access for veterans to non-VA healthcare, it will be extremely important that there is a continuity of care and that health records can be transferred seamlessly, and that is part of what you were talking about, I guess, when you were trying to do a quality check on the PC3 and finding those community providers. What can we do to ensure that this happens?

Dr. Lynch. I think that is a very good question, and it is a challenge. Right now our community providers do not have ready access to the VA's electronic health record. I can't tell you as we move forward and establish more permanent relationships whether we can begin to give certain providers access to the VA healthcare system. When I was in Omaha, we were able to do that for several of our community providers who gave regular service to the VA.

Mr. Takano. Well, you know, I know that as part of the ACA and the High Tech Act, which passed around the same time Congress created incentives for healthcare providers to make the transition to electronic healthcare records. Do you have any idea if this digitization has been done with interoperability with electronic health record systems already in place at the VA, the VistA system?

Dr. Lynch. I am going to defer to Dr. Clancy on that question, if I may.

Dr. Clancy. I will say that complying with the standards set out by meaningful use, is the popular term for those sets of incentives from CMS, although VA does not get money from CMS, but we are actually complying with all those standards, yes.

Mr. Takano. But the private healthcare providers, which who were given incentives to digitize their records --

Dr. Clancy. Correct.

Mr. Takano. -- is the standard set forth by CMS, will that provide interoperability with VistA?

Dr. Clancy. It should.

Mr. Takano. It should.

Dr. Clancy. Yes. And in some cases, we are starting to explore this, for example, with some pilot projects on allowing veterans for example, to get immunizations in a Walgreen's health facility. We can exchange that kind of information. So there is a difference between people meeting the same standards and being able to share freely across platforms, but that would be the ultimate goal.

Mr. Takano. So you are saying it should.

Dr. Clancy. Yes.

Mr. Takano. Theoretically, people, physicians who have been incentivized under the ACA to digitize, that those standards set forth, you said it was set forth by CMS, the --

Dr. Clancy. Yes.

Mr. Takano. -- digitization standards? That they should all -- that should provide the platform for interoperability with VistA?

Dr. Clancy. Yes. That certainly provides the first foundation for it.

Mr. Takano. So part of being able to facilitate this ability to access -- for our veterans to access care in the private arena would be to facilitate this interoperability, and so maybe part of the answer, Dr. Lynch, would be that if there were further incentives for our physicians to digitize to those standards, that this would be one part of the problem -- one part of the solution, interoperability?

Dr. Clancy. I guess I would say that this is a very strong priority for HHS right now, both CMS and the Office of the National Coordinator, and we are actively part of that strategic planning effort in terms of how do we accelerate the path towards interoperability, but that would make it much, much easier.

Right now what community partners do is they send a report, PC3 makes this a little bit easier because it is a condition of their getting paid, and that gets attached into the Vista record essentially as a portable downloadable file.

Mr. Takano. Would this incentivizing through PC3 be helpful if we put it also an incentive for them to digitize?

Dr. Clancy. That might be an option down the road for sure.

Mr. Takano. Great. Thank you.

The CHAIRMAN. Mr. Bilirakis, you are recognized for 5 minutes.

Mr. Bilirakis. Thank you, Mr. Chairman. I appreciate it very much.

Sir, Dr. Lynch, of the 70,000 veterans who were contacted that were on the waiting list, and the point is to remove them from the waiting list -- well, first of all, how many were contacted and they actually spoke to a person, a VA person, or -- tell me what the contact was, did they have an actual conversation with them?

Dr. Lynch. We don't have that breakdown yet Congressman, we will. There were attempts made to contact all veterans. The process is that there were three attempts made. If we could not contact the veteran, they then received a certified letter.

We will be developing the data as we collect it, and we should be able to provide you with the information that would tell you how many patients were directly contacted, how many patients were contacted by mail, how many patients could we not contact, and also the disposition of the patients contacted --

Mr. Bilirakis. Okay. If they received --

Dr. Lynch. -- did they wish to receive VA care or not?

Mr. Bilirakis. If they received something in the mail and they contacted the VA, would they speak to someone immediately?

Dr. Lynch. That would be my expectation, because --

Mr. Bilirakis. But you don't have any data on that?

Dr. Lynch. I don't have the data right now, no.

Mr. Bilirakis. Okay. Now, what about as far as the waiting time? So they contacted somebody, let's say, the contact was made, there was a conversation between a VA individual and the patient, the veteran. How long would they have to wait for an appointment?

Dr. Lynch. The expectation is that we would explain to them how long they would have to wait for care in VA. If they did not find that acceptable, we would provide care for them in the community.

Mr. Bilirakis. Okay. Now, you don't have any information to give me so far, any results as far as, let's say that they had to wait within, you know, how long would they have to wait to get a VA appointment within the VA?

Dr. Lynch. I don't have that information, but the expectation would be that if we could not see them within 30 days, we would offer them care in the community.

Mr. Bilirakis. Where did this 30-day period come from, this expectation, this policy?

Dr. Lynch. At the moment, there is not science behind it. There is evidence that in the community, patients are waiting anywhere from 15 to 30 days or longer to see care, and so I believe we chose that as a reasonable number. It does depend --

Mr. Bilirakis. Who chose that?

Dr. Lynch. VA chose that. It does depend on the acuity of the patient. If the patient needs to have care immediately, we would provide that. If there was an urgency, we would provide it within 30 days or offer it in the community.

I might turn to Dr. Clancy and ask if she has any further insight on the ability for the community to provide care in a more timely fashion than 30 days.

Dr. Clancy. Well, I would guess, Congressman, that you and your colleagues have probably seen data from recently released surveys of how long it takes to get a new patient appointment, which ranges from somewhere 10 days or a little bit less in Dallas, up to 45 or so in Boston. Obviously doesn't have a lot to do with the number of doctors in the area, because Boston has a lot of doctors.

The problem is there is no industry standard. I will say that when veterans contact the facility and are given a wait time or an expected wait time, and if that is not acceptable an option to go out into the community, they are also counseled that if they have a more urgent need, that they should come into an urgent care, or an emergency room for more immediate care.

Mr. Bilirakis. On the average, how long would it take if, let's say, it is decided they have to go outside the VA for care, how long it would take for them to -- the patient to get the appointment?

Dr. Clancy. A lot of that is going to depend on what existing capacity is in that community, so --

Mr. Bilirakis. On the average?

Dr. Clancy. We don't --

Mr. Bilirakis. The average patient?

Dr. Clancy. -- have a number for that yet. In the Dallas area, it would be much faster, given the data I just mentioned a moment ago that wait times there are shorter. I would expect it would be much, much tougher in the Boston area, for example.

Dr. Lynch. However, I would just add that with the PC3 contract, it is the contractual expectation that patients will be seen within 30 days.

Mr. Bilirakis. Okay. Yeah. One last question, Mr. Chairman.

Under the Department of Veterans Affairs Healthcare Programs Enhancement Act of 2001, the VA is mandated to establish a nationwide staffing policy for all VA medical facilities. Can you briefly describe what that policy is? Specifically, how does VA medical centers know which positions are needed, who they report that information to, and what is done with that information to address the staffing shortage?

Dr. Lynch. Congressman, I will have to take that for the record. I am not familiar with that policy or the data associated with that policy. I know that we currently have information through our Office of Productivity, Efficiency and Staffing that is looking at the number of physicians that we have, the specialty of those physicians and their ability to provide care in an efficient fashion using the RVU model.

Mr. Bilirakis. Please report back to me, because I feel you should have that information with you now today.

Mr. Bilirakis. So anyway, thank you very much.

Mr. Chairman, I yield back.

The CHAIRMAN. Thank you.

Mr. Walz, you are recognized for 5 minutes.

Mr. Walz. Well, thank you, Mr. Chairman. And thank you both for joining us again.

I am going to start out and just, as the chairman made note of this, a lot of this stems from just the inability to get information and for us to do our constitutionally-mandated job.

Over 3 weeks ago now we sat in here, and after the audits, several of our members here mentioned our facilities were flagged, and we were guarantied we would be told why that was. Nothing has been said and every day I get calls asking, what is wrong with these facilities? So I will ask all you, why don't you take that back and let them know we are waiting.

Dr. Lynch. Congressman, I actually had a discussion with Mr. Matkovsky before I came down here tonight. We knew this issue would be raised.

Mr. Walz. That is good foresight. I appreciate that you are thinking ahead that it is --

Dr. Lynch. He and I agreed that it is important that we brief the committee, and we will be making arrangements to do that, and then also provide briefings to other congressional staffs on a VISN by VISN basis.

Mr. Walz. Dr. Lynch, I think, and you have been coming down here a lot and I am very appreciative of the work you do, and as so many others, but I think the time has come when you know you don't get the benefit of the doubt on anything right now and after today's OSC, you mentioned that that was an unacceptable situation. Basically we had a veteran for 8 years that we warehoused. I would call that a national tragedy more than unacceptable.

And I guess for me, I am trying to get at the heart of this. I still think we are flirting around the edges here instead of getting at this. I am going to come back to this leadership and structure issue. If I asked a director of a medical center what our national strategy on veterans was, how would they answer?

Dr. Lynch. I hope they would answer that our strategy is to provide timely care to our veterans that is quality care --

Mr. Walz. Is that a strategy or a goal?

Dr. Lynch. It is probably a goal.

Mr. Walz. So if I am -- and I will go back to this from a national security standpoint. We have a national security strategy, we have the Quadrennial Defense Review, and then that identifies requirements and then DOD and the directed forces come back to fill those requirements. Do you do that at VA? Because I am getting back to this, that we have been trying this issue since 2005 on measuring capacity. Actually, I went back. We started in the 1980s. And so my question is, I am not convinced if I walked into Dallas or Minneapolis or Sioux Falls that I would get a strategy answer.

Dr. Lynch. I think, sir, I can offer that we are developing a strategy as it relates to access and as it relates to scheduling. We have in place a seven-step process that we are developing that will address the issue of accelerating care, that will address the development of demand capacity models, that will develop the policies and directives to drive scheduling and access.

That will relook at our performance assessment measures so that we can develop the measures and the goals appropriate to drive our system to the appropriate end point, which is quality, timely care. We are developing the processes to put together program oversight and integrity, to recruit people and to train them, and to integrate our care processes with the non-VA care model when necessary to meet --

Mr. Walz. Where does that guidance come from?

Dr. Lynch. Sir, this is an organizational plan that was developed within VHA over the last 3 to 4 weeks in response to the issues that we have faced regarding veteran access.

Mr. Walz. Is there White House input into any of this?

Dr. Lynch. Not to my knowledge, sir.

Mr. Walz. I want to have a specific one on this as we look at this care model, I want to give you an example that I went and did a little research over the last week in preparing for this, and there is a Mayo Clinic Phoenix down there, and prior to all this coming out, it was brought to my attention that they were doing some of the prostate surgeries in a fee for service, that they had that capacity. Is that correct?

Dr. Lynch. That is my understanding.

Mr. Walz. Now, what they said was is when they would have them come in, they would say, we can do the surgery in 48 hours. VA would say then, yeah, but we have to do the ECG's, and that will take 6 to 8 weeks, and so we had it going out into the community and we had a community partner ready to do it, and yet we went back in-house again to delay that care.

How will this be different? How will what you are doing now be different than that? If you have got prostate surgeons, urologists ready at Mayo Clinic, how are you still going to speed up the prep for that surgery, which is standard practice?

Dr. Lynch. Part of our non-VA care process would allow those providers to do certain basic studies that are essential to their either clinical assessment or pre-operative evaluation outside.

Mr. Walz. So the whole package will go?

Dr. Lynch. I would say that we would look at very high-cost studies, but routine studies should certainly be done in the community, not brought back to the VA.

Mr. Walz. Okay. I yield back. Thank you, Mr. Chairman.

The CHAIRMAN. Thank you, Mr. Walz.

Dr. Benishek, you are recognized for 5 minutes.

Mr. Benishek. Thank you, Mr. Chairman.

I liked your questions, Mr. Waltz.

Mr. Walz. Well, thank you, Dr. Benishek.

Mr. Benishek. It very much concerns me in the whole management system of the VA, the whole structure of it to me is really -- needs to be reevaluated, and I hope we can get to that, you know, at least move in that direction, because what is happening here is just not right.

A couple of ideas that came up from your testimony here today, Dr. Lynch is, you mentioned the fact that you weren't sure how much of this out -- you know, the community-based healthcare is proper, and it should be a temporary thing or a full thing, or should be kept in the VA, because it, you know, the extra expense associated with the private sector care, but then it occurs to me that I don't think you have any idea what it actually costs to take care of a patient within the VA. I mean, you know, in the private sector, basically we are talking about paying them at Medicare rates, but you don't have any idea if you are actually caring for veterans, at what rate it is costing us, do you?

Dr. Lynch. The VA actually does have a DSS model that does track the amount of cost that goes into the care of each patient. It hasn't been used extensively --

Mr. Benishek. You don't use it --

Dr. Lynch. -- but it is available at the medical centers --

Mr. Benishek. You don't use it for RVUs, like -- and if you are doing, you know, a certain code, you don't have any idea of like, how many RVUs you produce in the VA in a year for of the $50 billion for the VH healthcare system that we spend.

So we have a pretty good idea how many -- for Medicare, for example, how many units we are getting for the millions of dollars we are spending on Medicare, but I don't believe there is any comparison like that at the VA, so you don't really know if doing within the VA costs more money or doing it outside costs more money, do you?

Dr. Lynch. I do know that when I was in Omaha, we were able in our facility and across the network to begin looking at the cost of specific operations.

Mr. Benishek. Yeah, begin looking at does not mean you have an idea.

And another thing that I want to bring up -- oh, something that -- Mr. Takano, there is no interoperability amongst the electronic medical records. That does not exist. You can't get somebody's medical record from somewhere else just because you have electronic. That does not happen, it is impossible. I mean, that would be the ideal, but it doesn't work that way.

I have another question. The expectations of having this RVU unit and how many physicians you need and how much productivity they should have, are you aware that the VA has been informed that there has been a pipeline problem with physicians and the productivity problems for the last 30 years, and that the Inspector General eight times over the last 30 years has said that the VA needs to develop a plan, and it hasn't been done?

And last year when I had my subcommittee hearing, they told me it would be 3 years before there would be some kind of a plan to develop physician staffing? And then you talk about it a lot, but, I mean, I don't know how that would -- I don't know what you are actually going to do it?

Dr. Lynch. Congressman, that plan is in place. We will have productivity standards for all of our medical specialties by the end of this fiscal year.

Mr. Benishek. Well, I would like to see that, because when they testified, they said it would be 3 years before they had a staffing plan.

Dr. Lynch. They are about a year ahead of schedule.

Mr. Benishek. Well, I would like to -- can you please provide that? You know, in December 2012, there was a report by the IG that said that all the five facilities that the IG visited, were operating contrary to VA policy, which requires medical facilities to develop staffing plans that address performance measures, patient outcomes and other care indicators. So in December of 2012, they said that all the facilities they visited didn't operate according to VA policy; what has been done to change that?

Dr. Lynch. That is what the Office of Productivity, Efficiency and Staffing has been working on. Since the IG made those recommendations in late 2012, they have been developing the standards for each of our medical specialties.

Mr. Benishek. Do you know who is in charge of that?

Dr. Lynch. It is run by Dr. Carter Mecher works in that unit.

Mr. Benishek. Carter?

Dr. Lynch. Mecher.

Mr. Benishek. Mecher.

Dr. Lynch. M-e-c-h-e-r, and Eileen Moran.

Mr. Benishek. Okay.

Dr. Lynch. I believe they have been down and have testified, or not testified, but briefed some of the physicians of this committee.

Mr. Benishek. Well, it is just so -- you know, it is one thing to have a plan and then it is actually one thing to carry out the plan. So, I mean, the Inspector General told us back in this report that he went to five facilities, and none of the five facilities were carrying out, you know, the policy that was in place, and you don't have any idea, then, if anybody was, if any action was taken over the fact that these five places didn't --

Dr. Lynch. No, sir --

Mr. Benishek. -- comply with the rules --

Dr. Lynch. -- I don't.

Mr. Benishek. -- do you?

Dr. Lynch. I do not, sir.

Mr. Benishek. All right. I am out of time.

The CHAIRMAN. Yes, you are.

Ms. Brownley, you are recognized for 5 minutes.

Ms. Brownley. Thank you, Mr. Chairman. And thank you to the panel for being here this evening.

I wanted to talk a little bit about SCIP and so we obviously now have some new information that we have gleaned from the audit, and -- so when will the VA take in this new information that we have learned, you know, about the real wait times as opposed to the previously reported wait times and the increased demand thereof, and does the VA plan on updating the SCIP plan to reflect those new data points?

Dr. Lynch. The VA, as we are beginning to look at the information we have regarding productivity and our resources, is also seriously discussing the space needed to address the delivery of that care. That has been under active discussion this week, in fact.

Ms. Brownley. So if the VA is evaluating the capacity, space being one of them, I would imagine as you evaluate capacity, you are looking at space, the need for more personnel, in some cases it may be very extreme, you need much more space and many more personnel, and other places maybe it can be resolved by increasing hours at a particular facility.

Are you gathering all of that information and putting it in a matrix so that by each location across the country, we know exactly what the underlying issues are and how the VA will approach that, and most specifically, sort of timelines? I mean, space is something very concrete. Personnel might not be as concrete, but it is pretty concrete. You know, will you have that evaluation location by location and a timeline of which you believe you can accomplish what is needed?

Dr. Lynch. We already have most of that information location by location. We have physician information, we have staff support information, location by location. I cannot confirm whether we have space information, but it is critically important in making decisions regarding efficiency, and we are working and discussing the implications of space as we put our models together.

Ms. Brownley. So you will have a model of space, then, and timelines location by location, and you say you have -- you already have that for personnel? Is that what exists currently, or what exists currently and what is needed and the timeline?

Dr. Lynch. Yes and yes. We have the information based on what we currently have and we have been looking aggressively over the last several weeks at what may be required to either increase the efficiency of our providers, or if they are functioning efficiently, whether we need to consider adding additional physicians to meet that capacity.

Ms. Brownley. So could you share that information with me, then, on the personnel side?

Dr. Lynch. Certainly. Let me see if I can set up a briefing for you with the folks who put that together.

Ms. Brownley. Okay. And then on the -- what is your, I guess, timeline for space, what is your timeline to put together a matrix to identify what are the space needs throughout the country?

Dr. Lynch. I would have to get back to you on the space issue. That is still being discussed, and I don't have a definite timeline for that.

Ms. Brownley. Okay. The chairman in his opening comments talked about asking the question how quickly can the VA hire a doctor, and you talked about the fact that you weren't really sure, but I am wondering -- but you know it is too long. We all agree on that.

So can you just share with me just your -- at least the VA's initial thinking on what some of the barriers are and what might be some mechanisms for shortening that period and expediting the process?

Dr. Lynch. I think we are clearly going to have to work at improving the efficiency of our human resource process for handling new recruits. You are absolutely right: it is clearly too long, oftentimes we lose people during the process. Some of it is essential, the credentialing and privileging process is essential, but some of the other processes involved in human resources can clearly be improved in terms of their efficiency.

I think, interestingly, some of the things that we are learning in Phoenix as we are working with that facility to increase their capacity to add new physicians may help the rest of our system to function more efficiently in the HR process.

Ms. Brownley. Thank you.

I yield back.

The CHAIRMAN. Mr. Huelskamp, you are recognized for 5 minutes.

Mr. Huelskamp. Thank you, Mr. Chairman.

Dr. Lynch, as part of the VA's Accelerating Access to Care Initiative, you have committed to ensuring primary care clinic panels are correctly sized to achieve the desired productivity. What are these desired productivity standards that you are using for primary care providers?

Dr. Lynch. Right now the standards they are using are the number of patients per physician. They do have models that they can use to see whether we can increase that capacity based on staffing or based on room availability or based on patient complexity.

We are also beginning to implement the use of the productivity model to look at primary care and see if we can use that to take a look at not only the number of patients a physician is seeing, but the complexity of those patients and their productivity.

So, for instance, perhaps a physician is seeing six patients a day, perhaps they are new patients or complex patients that have a high relative value unit. That physician may actually be more productive than a physician who is seeing 15 established patients during the course of the day. So I think --

Mr. Huelskamp. And I do follow that. How do you monitor that, though?

Dr. Lynch. Right now we are monitoring that by looking at the RVU productivity of our physicians.

Mr. Huelskamp. Is that monitored at the national level, the vision level, the facility level?

Dr. Lynch. Yes, at the facility level.

Mr. Huelskamp. At the facility level. Now, given the gaming strategies and other things that have suggested or have shown that the data is not valid or maybe not reliable, do we have potentially the same problems with what you are attempting to measure here? Why would we not have similar problems with knowing exactly what is going on with productivity?

Dr. Lynch. Dr. Clancy?

Dr. Clancy. I think that is an incredibly important question and one that we share your concerns, and also recognize that since integrity of data has been a problem for us, we not only need to clean up our policies and streamline them, but that we also need to have some independent validation that these processes are both effective and that the integrity can be assured by an independent third party, and we will be doing just that.

RPTS MCCONNELL

DCMN CRYSTAL

[8:29 p.m.]

Mr. Huelskamp. So that has not been done?

Dr. Clancy. Not yet, because the scheduling new policy --

Mr. Huelskamp. So any of the data you have shared here has not been independently confirmed?

Dr. Lynch. The RVU data is validated based on what we are recovering from the way that physician activities --

Mr. Huelskamp. But if we have falsified data -- and we have shown that, the VA has admitted to that, the gaming strategies, 4 years ago admitted that was going on -- I don't know how the data could be valid or reliable in either case based on what Dr. Clancy just said. So I am trying to find out how you can assure me that the numbers you gave here actually match what is really happening in the real world.

Dr. Lynch. Congressman, point well taken. VA does need to establish the integrity of their data. I will take your comments back to the Office of Productivity, Efficiency and Staffing and ask them how we can validate the information we have so that we can establish the integrity of that data and assure you of the confidence that we have in that data.

Mr. Huelskamp. But the range you gave was 6 to 22 patients a day. That is your claim today?

Dr. Lynch. Yes, sir.

Mr. Huelskamp. That is not valid?

Dr. Lynch. I think that information is valid. I think it is very difficult to try to figure out --

Mr. Huelskamp. I had a whistleblower has approached my office from a facility -- and I am in my congressional district in four different VISNs, we are lucky that way, I guess -- but claims that there are primary care physicians that see as few as five patients in an entire day. That would be definitely outside the range. Could that be possible?

Dr. Lynch. I would have to look at the information and evaluate it. At this point, anything could be possible. And I am certainly willing to look at anything --

Mr. Huelskamp. I agree. And that is my problem here. When you say anything can be possible, this is not independently confirmed, but how do you make decisions when you don't know if your data is accurate? And, you know, gaming strategies, we have heard, actually the falsifying data, and what I have heard from this whistleblower. And there are some really hard-working physicians out there, but there are some that are working very, very hard, and then physicians across the hallway that see five patients a day, which basically half the day they are sitting there waiting for something. And obviously, when we are looking at ways to provide better access to care, ways we can do that by enhancing productivity, but we don't have the data, I think, to answer any of these questions.

And so I look forward to you showing us how the data is valid and reliable.

Mr. Huelskamp. But if this whistleblower identifies physicians that are not working as hard as they should be, we have got a serious problem in the system.

Dr. Lynch. Congressman, I think we need to understand that further.

Mr. Huelskamp. Okay. Thank you, Mr. Chairman. I yield back.

The CHAIRMAN. Dr. Ruiz, you are recognized for 5 minutes.

Mr. Ruiz. Thank you, Mr. Chairman.

The discussion on ways that technology and innovation can increase the capacity of the VA to provide timely, accessible, and high quality veteran-centered care is very important. However, today this committee learned that the Office of Special Counsel, whose job it is to protect whistleblowers and investigate their claims, found that the VA has failed to use information from whistleblowers to correct troubling patterns of deficiency of patient care that negatively impact the health and safety of our veterans, and they failed to correct these troubling patterns of these deficient patient-care practices. They describe quote, "A culture of non-responsiveness," unquote. The OSC revealed that the VA's Office of the Medical Inspector frequently refused to acknowledge the systematic problems in the VA that exist or acknowledge how they negatively affect veteran care. In other words, it was an institution-centered and not a veteran-centered response.

We need to create a veteran-centered culture of responsiveness. The Office of the Medical Inspector of the VA needs to either come forward with a serious explanation or get out of the way so solutions can be found and implemented and veterans can receive the care they need when they need it.

Today we are talking about accelerating access to care. What we need is an accelerated access to high-quality care, not inadequate care. My question is, how are you ensuring that the care to veterans is high quality? You know, as a physician in clinical practice, we have quality review mechanisms, and some of these mechanisms begin with credentialing, board certification, risk management, continuing medical education requirements, an evaluation of patient requests, and also chart audits. What systematic method are you ensuring from your healthcare providers or the system in order to ensure high-quality care?

Dr. Lynch. Congressman, I am going to defer to Dr. Clancy to answer that question.

Dr. Clancy. So you often hear it said that once veterans can get in they often think that the quality of care is very good. And in fact, by the numbers, whether you are looking at information reported to Hospital Compare, we use the same metrics, or the same metrics that are used to evaluate health plans, as a system VHA looks quite good.

In addition to that, at a very high level we have all of the regulations that the private sector has, plus additional investigations by the Inspector General, the GAO, and other parties. So we have quite a bit of oversight in that regard.

VA, before there was a famous Institute of Medicine report on not harming patients, "To Err is Human," actually stood up a National Center for Patient Safety. As a result of that and other efforts, there is a very, very strong focus on psychological safety and encouraging all employees to step forward. If you see something, say something -- we actually have a video about this that has been shown widely -- stop the line. And I think Secretary Gibson was very, very clear with respect to whistleblowers where you started out here today in accepting the Office of Special Counsel report.

Mr. Ruiz. So I think that there are definitely good practices, and Loma Linda University is one of the better VA hospitals in our country and they serve the veterans in my district. However, even amongst the best, there are always issues that we need to improve. And if there is a report saying that there is a culture of unresponsiveness to these grave scenarios that is systematic, then I think that we need to get to the bottom of it and figure out where that disconnect between the whistleblowers and the responsiveness of those responsible to make sure that these practices don't happen.

Let me get to the next question. Do we have a count of full-time equivalent primary care physicians per veteran ratio within the VISNs?

Dr. Lynch. Yes, I am sure we do.

Mr. Ruiz. Do you know what it is?

Dr. Lynch. It would vary by VISN.

Mr. Ruiz. Of course.

Dr. Lynch. I would have to get you the specific information for VISN or for a facility.

Mr. Ruiz. And are they used to determine where your resources are spent?

Dr. Lynch. They are certainly used in association with information regarding demand to make resource decisions, yes, sir.

Mr. Ruiz. The national recommendation is one full-time equivalent physician per 2,000 Americans. To be considered medically underserved, it is one full-time equivalent physician per 3,500. So it would be important to determine whether a physician-per-veteran ratio reveals an underserved VA system per area so that we can start addressing these underserved areas with priority.

Thank you. I believe that is the end of my time, and I yield back my time.

The CHAIRMAN. Thank you very much, Doctor.

Mr. Coffman, you are recognized for 5 minutes.

Mr. Coffman. Thank you, Mr. Chairman.

Dr. Lynch, how long have you been with the VA system?

Dr. Lynch. About 30 years, sir.

Mr. Coffman. How long have been in senior leadership with the VA system?

Dr. Lynch. About a year-and-a-half.

Mr. Coffman. About a year-and-a-half. And what surprises me, and I certainly commend the VA for having this Access to Care Initiative, I think the problem is, and I think we need to be convinced, because what we are asking is the same people that drove us into this ditch to figure out how to get us out of this ditch.

And what amazes me is the fact that under the leadership within the VA, all of the issues have come forward through whistleblowers. And I know that you went, when the story I think that was the catalyst for all of this, which was the Phoenix VA scandal, and I think you personally went down there to look at it, I mean, you didn't talk --

Dr. Lynch. I have been to Phoenix four times.

Mr. Coffman. Well, when you testified before this committee, you went there, you came back, you didn't talk to the schedulers that were actually doing the work. You didn't talk to Dr. Foote, the key whistleblower. You made no outreach to him. And you didn't talk to any veterans, and you testified to that effect here.

And so we are counting on you to get us out of the ditch. I just don't think it is going to happen. I just don't think you can do it. And I think what we need is we need a new Secretary of the Veterans Affairs that is going to come in and is going to clean house. Because you have been in the system for a long time, and you are not outraged. The reality is, you are not outraged. And you have testified before this committee a number of times; always been defensive, always been defensive. Covering, concealment, escape, and evasion, those are terms I learned in the military as a ground combat officer. And you have used those brilliantly, I think, before this committee. And the VA has not been transparent. It has admitted a lack of integrity.

So tell us how we can count on you and the leadership team that exists there now to get us out of this ditch and to be honest with this committee and with the American people, with the veterans that you are here to serve.

Dr. Lynch. Congressman, I value the VA system greatly. I think it is a good system.

Mr. Coffman. Well, it is not a good system. How could you say, tell me how you could say it is a good system.

Dr. Lynch. I think it is a good system, Congressman.

Mr. Coffman. Really?

Dr. Lynch. Yes, I do.

Mr. Coffman. Not if you are a veteran, it is not a good system.

Dr. Lynch. I think it provides good quality care. I think Dr. Clancy can confirm --

Mr. Coffman. Not there. Here is the problem.

Dr. Lynch. Our system compares favorably with the private sector in terms of quality of care and in patient satisfaction. I think that, yes, we are challenged right now. We are challenged because of data integrity. And we certainly need to re-earn the confidence of the public, of the Congress, and of our veterans, and we are working to do that, sir.

Mr. Coffman. You are just glossing this stuff over.

Dr. Lynch. I am not glossing over --

Mr. Coffman. I mean, you ought to outraged. It is not a good system. It is not serving the needs of our veterans.

Dr. Lynch. I take this all very seriously.

Mr. Coffman. And you are part of the problem. I just don't see you as part of the solution. I don't see you able to get us out of this ditch, and we are in a ditch, and you are in denial that we are in the ditch.

Dr. Lynch. Congressman, I am not denying at all that we have a significant problem. If you want to call it a ditch I will not disagree with you.

Mr. Coffman. We just had testimony --

Dr. Lynch. I think we do have a way forward. I think we do have plans. I think we do need to reestablish our integrity. I think we can do that. And I think we can salvage a system which does provide good care and we can make that system provide timely access.

Mr. Coffman. I am absolutely stunned that you would call this, with all of the information that has come out, and I don't think we are at the bottom of all of this yet, that you would call this a good system I think is absolutely stunning. And I think that the Veterans Administration is the most mismanaged agency of the Federal Government. And I think that it has not been there to serve those who have served this country, but the leadership of the VA has been there to serve themselves.

And we had testimony before this committee about all the bonuses, all the bonuses, despite the incredible bureaucratic incompetence and cultural of corruption. That is the only thing you all seem to be effective in, is writing checks to each other.

Mr. Chairman, I yield back.

The CHAIRMAN. Mrs. Kirkpatrick, you are recognized for 5 minutes.

Mrs. Kirkpatrick. Thank you, Mr. Chairman. And I want to thank you and Ranking Member Michaud for continuing to have these hearings. I feel like we are not getting to the bottom of this.

And, Dr. Lynch, we have had a number of hearings. You have been here a number of times. And I just want to focus on the scheduling delays. That is the problem that we are trying to get to the bottom of. But we have heard, this committee has heard that there are five reasons for these scheduling delays: that there was an unexpected surge of new patients; there was not enough funding; obsolete facilities and obsolete technology; a lack of patient extenders and personnel; a lack of consistent policy across the system.

But that just further describes a problem, and my question is, why? Why did the VA not anticipate a surge in new patients when we know that we have an aging population. Why did the VA not have enough funding when we have given them all of the funding that they have requested?

And so we are starting to think as a committee that this is a systemic problem, but we are still just not getting to the bottom of why. Can you answer that for me?

Dr. Lynch. I think part of the reason may be relatively self-evident. We were not getting good data from the system. We didn't have a good measure of those patients that were waiting.

Mrs. Kirkpatrick. But why? Why?

Dr. Lynch. I think we know why. I think we have acknowledged that the system was not honest. We were not getting the information we needed. We had performance measures that were misguided, and we need to reform that so we have accurate information and we can resource our system appropriately based on demand and capacity.

I think we have the tools to do that. I think we have the information to do that. We need to assure that our data is accurate. We are working very hard to do that. We are making demands on both our VISN directors and medical center directors to assure that the practices in their clinic are according to policy. We acknowledge that we are probably going to have to have an independent third party confirm that that information is accurate, because at the moment we have to verify to you, we have to justify to the American public that our information is real and accurate and we can provide timely care and we can give the information that we need to assess demand and capacity.

Mrs. Kirkpatrick. Well, I appreciate your answer, but I feel like we are still not getting to the bottom of this.

And let me just say, why is the VA so slow? Why are they so slow in responding to Mr. Walz's office? Why have they been so slow in responding to this committee. It is just why, why, why? Is it because there aren't enough --

Dr. Lynch. Congresswoman, I apologize for our slowness. It is not correct. I think we do have to work with this committee and we do have to work with Congress if we are going to build a better VA system. And we do need to give you the information that you need.

Mrs. Kirkpatrick. Dr. Lynch, let me ask you just one other. Is it a system that can innovate?

Dr. Lynch. Yes, I think it is a system that can innovate, and I think we have shown that we can innovate in the past, particularly in response to crisis. If you look back in the mid-1980s, there were concerns about surgical care in the VA. The VA developed a risk-adjusted model of outcomes assessment that has now become the model for the private sector. In the 1990s, the VA was criticized, and the VA innovated with the electronic health record. That has now become a standard for the private sector.

I think we can innovate and I think we have an opportunity here in VA to respond to this crisis with an innovative model of staffing, of assessing demand and capacity that can become a standard for the industry as well.

Mrs. Kirkpatrick. Please do it.

I yield back my time.

Dr. Clancy. Well, if I could just add one thing to what Dr. Lynch just said.

Mrs. Kirkpatrick. Okay.

Dr. Clancy. I think all of your questions are critically important, and frankly, are tearing us up as well. But right now we are focused 100 percent on trying to get veterans into the system and using all the tools available at our disposal. There will be time for the "why" questions and the much tougher analytical questions that all of you are asking about how do we fine-tune capacity and demand. But right now the number of veterans waiting is an emergency, and that gets the highest priority. That does not mean anything else is off the radar screen.

And I just have to say in response to the innovation question, I did have the pleasure and opportunity of visiting VISN 1, which happens to encompass the State of Maine, and some of the innovations that they have tested and deployed up there are really terrific. I think our challenge is figuring out how to spread it and to achieve the same successes as we have seen in surgery and in other areas.

Mrs. Kirkpatrick. Thank you. Thank you, Dr. Clancy.

The CHAIRMAN. Dr. Wenstrup, you are recognized for 5 minutes.

Mr. Wenstrup. Thank you, Mr. Chairman.

You know, as we sit here and talk about all this, I think a lot of times as people are watching it, it almost seems like we are talking about patients as through they are Monopoly pieces. And when Mr. Walz brings up the point of the possibility of getting surgery within 48 hours, but it is 6 weeks until they can get their preop work done at the VA, it is disappointing that that surgeon can't make something happen sooner, or that there is nowhere to go, that these types of things aren't corrected. And I am sure that these have gone on for years.

And there is a lot of things that we are hearing tonight, and you share our concerns. Well, when did you start? When I got here, I went to General Shinseki three times saying I would be willing as a physician to go into the clinics and go into the ORs -- I come from private practice, I trained at a VA -- and to discuss why it is so much slower, why there are so many fewer patients being seen. Never got a response. Never got action on that.

You talked about RVUs, and for our fans watching at home, they probably don't know what those are. Relative value units. And so a new patient has a higher value than an established patient. A short procedure has fewer value units than a long procedure, those types of things. So when people hear that, they know what we are talking about.

When did you start looking at the RVUs?

Dr. Lynch. The RVUs, I believe, became part of our evaluation process after the OIG report in late 2012.

Mr. Wenstrup. Okay, so just in the last couple of years. And, of course, that has been around for a while as some type of measure. But my question is, are you measuring how many RVUs per patients, per day, per month, per provider, per facility, per VISN?

Dr. Lynch. Yes, sir, we are.

Mr. Wenstrup. Okay. Well, that would be nice, because if you could just maybe pick one VISN and give me all that information tomorrow, I would appreciate seeing how you are going about doing that. I would be very curious.

Mr. Wenstrup. And Dr. Benishek brought up a very good point when he said, how much are you spending per RVU? So if you take all the money that you are spending on these patients and then tally up how many RVUs that have been built up, how much are you spending per RVU? Because I can tell you, Medicare knows how much they spend per RVU because it is already established. So your budget is out there. You are measuring RVUs, but not how much you are spending per RVU, and I think that is key. And I also think it is key that you look at how many patients a doctor is seeing each day, or a facility is seeing each day. There is more than one way to measure these types of things.

In our practice, if one doctor is seeing 60 patients and a similar doctor is seeing 30, we are talking to the one with 30 and see how we can help them get that up and continue the quality that they have to have. But when you are comparing to yourself, I don't think you are getting anywhere. And that is part of the problem.

So my next question is, when you talk about doing these evaluations of efficiency, who is doing this? Because if it is somebody that has been in the VA system their whole life they don't know what they are measuring, they don't compare to successful, healthy healthcare systems. So who is doing this currently?

Dr. Lynch. Right now it is being done by Dr. Carter Mecher and Eileen Moran.

Mr. Wenstrup. And are they from the private sector? Have they been in academia? Have they been in the VA? Where have they been through their careers that make them qualified to be very good at this?

Dr. Lynch. I don't know Dr. Mecher's history. I know that he has met with the physicians on this committee, so I think you have talked with him.

Mr. Wenstrup. Yes.

Dr. Lynch. I think he does have a good handle and a good understanding of the RVU system and productivity. I think he has some very innovative concepts of how we can use that to resource our system and to look at rightsizing the number of physicians and the capacity that we have.

Mr. Wenstrup. And that is helpful, but I would definitely look at someone who has had great success in these areas, and they exist throughout our country without a doubt.

Dr. Clancy. I would just add that we are speaking to Kaiser and a number of leaders from private sector systems, and if you had other suggestions we would be all ears.

Mr. Wenstrup. Well, and those are good suggestions. And I would also suggest that you encourage the President and the Senate to confirm someone who has some administrative experience in the private sector in these areas. I think it would be a great benefit to our veterans and to our country.

And lastly, I do want to point out that the Cincinnati VA, I represent that area, has been flagged. I have asked for why they were flagged and have not received my notification yet as to why. And certainly somebody knows why. So I hope we get that very quickly as well. So I look forward to seeing one of those reports on the RVUs as well.

And I yield back. Thank you.

The CHAIRMAN. Ms. Kuster, you are recognized for 5 minutes.

Ms. Kuster. Thank you very much, Mr. Chairman.

And thank you, Dr. Lynch and Dr. Clancy, for being with us this evening.

I think what all of us are trying to do is to be helpful. I think our chair opened the hearing asking how can Congress help you? And our challenge is that this whole process feels like a Rubik's cube. Every time we think we have got a piece in order and we think we understand what the problem is, is it not enough physicians, then we offer to help on that, but maybe that is not the problem, it is a space problem. If it is not a space problem, it is the support staff. And the list goes on and on.

I am very fortunate to have experience with the VA in New Hampshire. My father-in-law got very excellent care within that system. But obviously the concern that we have is that that be replicated for every veteran around the country. So the focus of my comments is, how do we ensure access to high-quality care at a cost that the taxpayers can afford for every veteran?

And I have spent 25 years in the private sector on policy issues. I know this isn't easy, this conundrum of high-quality care, access, and cost is sometimes a wobbly three-legged stool. But in your case it seems that the problems of scheduling and wait time data has called into question the whole basis for your staffing and capacity calculations.

And I think, Dr. Lynch, you just mentioned it. You are trying to match supply and demand, but you don't have an accurate picture on the demand side, and so trying to determine what the staffing model would be is of limited use. And when you tell us the average is a physician seeing 10 patients a day, does that include the data that we have heard in this committee of 50 percent no-shows? So is that actually a physician that has 20 slots per day, but only 10 patients walk through the door?

And we want to help you with this. We want to get the policy right. We have legislation that we are offering this week, it will be bipartisan, that is about getting residents involved, give you greater capacity. We would be happy to help talk about what the space issues. But how can you help us with where to start helping you?

Dr. Lynch. Congresswoman, I think we can start by trying to give you the information that you ask for. And I apologize if you have not seen that. We have provided a briefing to members of this committee on the productivity model that we have.

I acknowledge that until we can assure the accuracy of our scheduling data that information is going to be flawed, although I am confident at this point that I think we do have reasonable information on productivity, and we can begin to use the productivity information to begin to look at what we need in the way of additional staffing to increase the efficiency of physicians, or in those practices that are very efficient, who we may need in the way of additional physicians.

So I think we have a start, but I think we need to gather more data. I think we need to have accurate data on access before we can come to a final answer.

Ms. Kuster. And then if we could add Dr. Benishek's analysis about the cost in-house and outside the VA because it is difficult for us to make that recommendation as to how to make these adjustments. We want veterans to be seen in a timely way, but it is not unlimited, the funds that can be put toward this. If it is less expensive within the VA, then let's expand your capacity. If it is less expensive outside the VA, then let's use private facilities. But we are not able to measure this at this point.

Dr. Clancy. No, but I think that all of the information that you have heard and we look forward to briefing you more on, on the productivity and staffing, will be a huge puzzle piece here that will be foundational to getting to this second order question, after the emergency of addressing people waiting in line right now, about what kinds of resources do we need.

And the issues that Dr. Lynch brought up a couple of times about a make-or-buy decision at the very local level because that is where it needs to happen, the answer to that is not going to be thumbs up, thumbs down all the way. It is probably going to be make in some areas, primary care, for example, and buy in some other specialty areas, and so forth. And a lot of that will be a very dynamic relationship with community capacity and so forth.

Ms. Kuster. My time is up, but I do have a specific question I would like to get to later about women being served in the VA, because I think that is a unique situation as well, and problematic at best.

So thank you, Mr. Chair. I yield back.

The CHAIRMAN. Mrs. Walorski, you are recognized for 5 minutes.

Mrs. Walorski. Thank you, Mr. Chairman.

Dr. Lynch, I would like to ask a question about the VA staffing and productivity standards. The IG that was here a couple of weeks ago made an interesting kind of assessment. He pretty much said be careful what you wish for to our committee in this issue of fee-basis care versus VA care. So I did some investigation in my State. I learned there are a number of VA hospitals, including the one in Fort Wayne, Indiana, the VA medical center, that are not functioning at full capacity, they are turning patients away, sending them to non-VA hospitals due to a lack of appropriate staffing or facilities.

In this case, the Fort Wayne VA, their ICU is closed. The ER is now using criteria over what patients they will accept and those they will turn away based on their facilities. By paying for non-VA care in addition to operating half-empty hospitals, VA appears to be paying for two systems of care. So do you know how many VA hospitals fit this description?

Dr. Lynch. I don't.

Mrs. Walorski. Can you give me that number? I mean, I found the Fort Wayne one pretty quickly.

Dr. Lynch. I think there are facilities that we are struggling, they are older facilities, not always like Fort Wayne where they are in larger communities. Sometimes they are in smaller communities. The population that they support is small and oftentimes it is difficult for them to support an ICU. Those are difficult decisions. But we need to look at our facilities, where they are, and we need to assure that we are using them optimally.

Mrs. Walorski. And then I guess my follow-up question would be what the IG warned us about, which is, who is looking at those numbers to figure out? For example, in Fort Wayne, those numbers for fee-basis care are skyrocketing every year. Well, once I looked at that and found out there is no ICU and they are using criteria who they can take and who they can't take, they may have to send somebody across the street for some kind of a risk-basis procedure because there is no ICU.

So who looks at those numbers? Is that just a regional, statewide, or just that specific hospital looks at those skyrocketing numbers? And at someplace who makes the assessment of, are we paying for two facilities or are we paying for one?

Dr. Lynch. So part of the challenge we have is that, based on the volume in some of our facilities, we cannot support an ICU, not because we can't afford it, because we don't have the patient volume to maintain competence. And so there is a balance, and oftentimes it is felt that because of the volume and because of the competence, it is better to send these patients into the private sector.

I understand your concern, and we do need to look at where our costs are going and how we are using our facilities.

Mrs. Walorski. We do need to look at, or is somebody actively looking at this now that all this information really is coming to us from the Inspector General? Is somebody ongoing going to look at that to see this cost-benefit analysis of what are we paying for, are we paying for two systems, or is that something you are going to look at in the future?

Dr. Lynch. I don't know whether we have an active exercise in place, but we certainly do need to have one moving forward.

Mrs. Walorski. And I just got a note from a constituent that says there must be some kind of a CNN program on tonight and that there is a new revelation. It says, ''Records of dead veterans were changed or physically altered, some even in recent weeks, to hide how many people died while waiting for care at the Phoenix VA hospital, a whistleblower told CNN in stunning revelations that point to a new coverup in the ongoing VA scandal. 'Deceased' notes on files were removed to make statistics look better so veterans would not have to be counted as having died while waiting for care.'' And the quote is from Pauline DeWenter.

So you have been to the Phoenix facility four times. Are you aware of this new revelation?

Dr. Lynch. I am not aware of the revelation. I am aware that the OIG is looking carefully at all of the deaths that occurred. I do not know of any attempts to hide deaths, Congresswoman.

Mrs. Walorski. And I guess my follow-up question to this, because I am guessing this is going to be big news in the morning, or probably big news tonight when our constituents are all watching their late news, but again it is so hard, I guess to echo the comments on this committee, it is so hard to take the information seriously that you give us tonight when there are these ongoing investigations by new whistleblowers that they are taking stickers off of files, removing names still, while we have been doing these hearings for a couple of months, and Americans are literally wondering, when is this going to stop? This looks like a new revelation tonight.

Under all the scrutiny, all the lights, all the spirit of full disclosure, Phoenix is still doing this kind of stuff, and you guys have had them under a microscope, and you have physically been there four times, and this is new?

Dr. Lynch. Congresswoman, I don't know the details of the accusation.

Mrs. Walorski. Could you provide that to us? I think the details are out, but could you provide us the VA answer to that in a timely manner?

Dr. Lynch. I will certainly try as I understand it.

Mrs. Walorski. Thank you, Mr. Chairman. I yield back my time.

The CHAIRMAN. Mr. O'Rourke, you are recognized for 5 minutes.

Mr. O'Rourke. Thank you, Mr. Chairman.

Dr. Lynch, you mentioned earlier that $312 million has been made available to accelerate access to care to veterans who have been unable to receive it thus far. Where did that money come from?

Dr. Lynch. The money was recovered from funds that were not being used across VA. I believe that there was some activation moneys that was repurposed to cover the Accelerated Care Initiative.

Mr. O'Rourke. And what are activation moneys?

Dr. Lynch. Activation moneys are sometimes moneys that are used for new projects. I don't know the details, but I would assume that it was felt that the moneys were not absolutely necessary at this time and could be repurposed to address the immediate concern, which was the provision of timely care to veterans.

Mr. O'Rourke. And will you or the VA be coming back to Congress to recover those moneys after we get through this crisis?

Dr. Lynch. I don't think that is our intention, Congressman.

Mr. O'Rourke. Okay.

Dr. Lynch. I think our immediate attention is to provide timely access to care, and at the moment we are trying to use the funds that we have.

Mr. O'Rourke. What I am trying to get at, and I agree with you that that should be our focus, and I appreciate Dr. Clancy saying that earlier that, that the number one priority before us is to connect veterans who need care to those providers who can give it to them, but I do want to get to the chairman's question and one that my colleague, Ms. Kuster, brought up, which is, what will you be likely be asking for from Congress?

I think this is a time where the American people and their representatives here would be very open to a request from the VA to say, to get to the level of care that we have promised to our veterans we need X. And you say that you have provided $312 million. Is there more to be found among those funds from which you have taken it so far? Will there be more needed in the coming days? I mean, we are really only weeks out from the revelations, and as Mrs. Walorski pointed out and others, myself included, in our districts we are still finding new gaps and shortfalls that need to be met.

So I am thinking, and you may not have a number in mind, but wouldn't you say that you are likely going to come back to Congress to request additional funds?

Dr. Lynch. I can't answer that question right now. I can tell you that we are beginning to look at the resources, particularly personnel resources that we need to increase our capacity, and we will be working with the Congress to develop a proposal that would allow us to hire more personnel to provide that care.

I know that we are looking carefully at the money we are spending on fee-basis services. We have been able to find some central money to send those patients out. Facilities and networks have also been able to identify moneys as well. It is anticipated that we will probably increase VA funding on fee-basis care from about $4.8 billion to about $5.4 billion this year.

Mr. O'Rourke. And I would also ask you to, and you essentially committed to this earlier in previous answers, but pay special attention to the providers that we have within the VA system today and retaining them there. When I met with providers in El Paso a couple of months ago morale could not have been lower, and a lot of it had to do with the amount that they were being paid, seeing so many of their colleagues leave service within the VA to work with DOD, which paid more, to work within the private sector, which paid more. In some cases they were single parents. These are nurses, nurse practitioners, providers of all kinds.

And I have just got to think that as you are repurposing these funds and perhaps asking more from Congress, I think it is really important that we ensure that we are attracting the absolute best within the VA system that we are actually then able to retain them. One primary health provider told of prescribing for mental health patients and seeing the mental health caseload that is coming in there, which he said he didn't feel good about at all. He said, this is not right, but I am not going to let that person go untreated even though I wasn't trained to treat somebody for these kind of problems. That raises a number of questions and issues in itself, but it gets back to this issue of resources for providers.

I have a number of other questions specific to El Paso, but we will continue to reach out to you in between these hearings and at these hearings to follow up when we don't get an answer. I appreciate your responsiveness so far. And I do ask Dr. Clancy and Dr. Lynch and the leadership, as we get through this immediate crisis, if we lose this opportunity to address the real systemic, structural, cultural problems within the VA, I think that we will be right back here again in another couple of years, 5 years, 10 years, having this very same discussion.

So while addressing care and connecting veterans to care is important, let's make sure that we don't stop there. We need to address the culture, the operations, and the system. So anyhow, thank you for your answers and your work on this.

And, Mr. Chair, I yield back.

The CHAIRMAN. Thank you very much.

Mr. Jolly, you are recognized for 5 minutes.

Mr. Jolly. Thank you, Mr. Chairman.

Dr. Lynch, I want to give credit where credit is due. I recently hosted in my congressional district what I call the VA intake day, invited the community to come in and talk about their care, their compliments, their concerns at both Bay Pines and Haley. We had about 300 people come in, and I will tell you, we had a lot of people come in simply to defend the VA health care that they receive.

The other thing I want to compliment you on is Secretary Gibson said several weeks ago the Department was in the process of contacting 90,000 people who were on a waiting list. I actually heard from people in my district who had been contacted by phone. One of them was told, your dermatology appointment is 4 months away, and if you would like, we can move that up and fee you out.

So I want to compliment the Department for that, yourself, the Secretary as well.

I will also tell you just as a matter of a metric, we gave a questionnaire to folks, and for those of the 200 that filled out surveys, of those who had sought to go outside the system for non-VA care, fully 50 percent rated that experience in trying to get the VA to fee them out as either poor or very poor, expressing a lot of frustrations with the ability to get outside the system. It was a self-selected group. I recognize that. Those were some quick metrics we got.

Mr. O'Rourke mentioned mental health and behavioral health. Over Memorial Day I was approached by a mom whose son had committed suicide while he was waiting for mental health services. The fiscal year 2014 MILCON-VA bill directed the Department to competitively contract with non-VA providers in certain communities where there was a need for additional mental and behavioral health capacity, as well as where there was also a non-VA infrastructure that could actually provide that.

Are you aware of that direction, and can you update us on whether or not that has been pursued or is in the process of being implemented?

Dr. Lynch. I know that the VA has been actively working with the community. They have been holding almost on a yearly basis mental healthcare summits to inform the community of opportunities to participate in the care of veterans. So I think we are moving aggressively to involve the community where they are available in the care of veterans if it is necessary.

Mr. Jolly. I understand that reflects a spirit. But the Department was directed by the Congress. Congress determines the budget. Congress makes directions when it comes to how that money is to be spent. And in the 2014 bill, Congress directed the Department, didn't ask, directed the Department to have a demonstration project to competitively contract out in certain communities, at the choosing of the VA, mental and behavioral health non-VA care to do a demonstration project, to relieve capacity in certain areas. I guess particularly given the position you have, are you aware of that in the 2014 budget?

Dr. Lynch. Yes, I am aware of that.

Mr. Jolly. And has anything been done to implement that?

Dr. Lynch. Yes, it has.

Mr. Jolly. What has been done?

Dr. Lynch. We have developed demonstration projects, I believe, at five or six of our facilities to involve the community in veteran care, and we are evaluating the results. That is in process, yes.

Mr. Jolly. Okay. I would very parochially tell you how wonderful the Bay Pines and Haley system is, and the fact that stone claw season starts in October and we have the best beaches in the world. So to the extent that Tampa fits that profile and the Pinellas County community, I would encourage you to look at it.

Two last questions. One, for non-VA care right now, those who ask to go outside, I understand that folks who need a specialty care service that is not available from within the VA are likely the most candidates. What about for the VA patients who simply aren't satisfied with the quality of care and ask to see a different primary physician outside the system? Is that ever accommodated through non-VA care?

Dr. Lynch. I think the VA would attempt to find the patient another provider within VA if he was unsatisfied with his current provider.

Mr. Jolly. Is there any -- and I understand there is some statutory guidance -- any feasibility of going outside of the VA?

Dr. Lynch. In rare instances, if the patient is very unhappy, and I am speaking from personal experience, as chief of staff, I had authorized patients to receive care outside the VA.

Mr. Jolly. Okay. And my last question. Mrs. Walorski just shared the story that is breaking, and I understand it is breaking. You haven't had an opportunity to review it. But I do have a very specific question, because the IG talked about criminal investigations, or investigating allegations that rose to the criminal level. We have had several hearings thus far. Were you, Dr. Lynch, personally aware that this was a matter being investigated, that the word "deceased" or the label "deceased" had been or was being removed from files? Did you have actual awareness of that, that that was being investigated?

Dr. Lynch. This is the first I have heard of it.

Mr. Jolly. So you weren't aware it was being investigated?

Dr. Lynch. No, I was not.

Mr. Jolly. Okay. Thank you very much. I appreciate it. Yield back.

The Chairman. Ms. Titus, you are recognized for 5 minutes.

Ms. Titus. Thank you, Mr. Chairman.

I would like to go back to a point that Ms. Kuster was making at the end of her comments. We are talking about evaluating the capacity of the VA to care for veteran patients. I want to look specifically at the VA's capacity to serve our female veterans. They are often referred to as the hidden veterans or the silent veterans because they are less likely to seek service because it is not very accommodating. And the statistics that have just come out in an AP story certainly show that.

With regard to capacity, last year the VA served 390,000 female vets, and yet a quarter of the VA hospitals do not have a full-time gynecologist on staff. A quarter. With regard to quality, half of the women veterans received medication through the VA healthcare system that could cause birth defects, despite the fact that many are of child-bearing age and the majority were not on contraception. This is much higher than would occur in the private practice.

With regard to care coordination, the VA OIG has said that 60 percent of female veterans at community clinics didn't receive the results of their normal breast cancer exam within the required 2 weeks, which is your own policy, and even more disturbingly, 45 percent of those results never made it into the electronic health records data system.

I mean, I find these statistics are as bad, if not worse than some of the others that we have been talking about just generally speaking, and they indicate that the issues of access to quality care and proper coordination of care may be even worse for our female veterans than they are for the general population.

Now, I understand you have some plan to ensure that there is a designated female provider, women's provider in each facility, so I would like to ask you, what is your timeline for achieving that goal? When are you going to start doing some training of VA providers on healthcare concerns like drugs that can cause birth defects? And just what is your plan for looking at the female population, because that is a group of veterans that is going to increase in number?

Dr. Clancy. You are absolutely right, Congresswoman, and I thank you for your questions. We were concerned by some of the findings reported in the story as well. About 80 percent of our facilities do have a designated women's health provider. And in some of the other facilities there has been a challenge identifying someone to do that, so we are looking into training some existing staff, for example some of the current primary care clinicians to be able to meet that role.

I should just point out this is not something that we just came up with on the spur of the moment for women. I mean, this is an area where we have had other similar sorts of experience training people with specialized expertise, for example when there is a particular problem that is much more common in one facility. We figured out how to bring specialist expertise to the primary care facility. We are going to be trying to do the same thing so that we can get up to 100 percent as soon as possible.

The issue on mammograms, as I understand it in terms of the timely follow-up, particularly for abnormal findings, has been the focus of some substantial improvement efforts, and we can get you more details on that.

Dr. Clancy. The other thing I would just point out in terms of women's health is that obviously women have issues that relate to their unique needs, and issues as women, as well as all the other stuff that human beings get, whether that is heart disease, lung disease, and so forth. VHA is the only system in this country that actually routinely reports publicly and transparently about how we do for women and men. That is not true for any other payors in this country. And in fact, the disparities are minimal to nonexistent between the care provided to women and men. I am talking mainstream heart disease and so forth. The issue of gynecological care is one that has improved quite substantially, but clearly we have more room to go.

Ms. Titus. I don't think that is accurate. I am glad it has been improving, but a recent opinion by the American Congress of OB-GYN says that there is urgent need to continue training providers in this area. And you mentioned that you have done some work with the reporting back, especially of abnormal results, and it says that they are typically informed within 3 days, and ''typically'' is in quotation marks, said that you don't really show how widely the improvements have been adopted or what specific progress has been made in this area. It is kind of hit or miss like so many of the things that we have been hearing about.

So I am concerned that you are just going to train primary caregivers to be experts on women's health. Maybe that is an interim measure, but it is certainly not the same as having somebody who is qualified in that field. And again, I go back to these clinics that exist, say in rural Nevada, where it is very hard to find somebody who is an expert, or even in our urban centers like Las Vegas where we lack providers. And this is something that we need to address.

Even if you send them out into the community, and then you don't track their results out in the private sector, or if you send them out and there are no providers in the private sector, we really have just kind of traded the devil for the witch. We haven't solved the problem.

Dr. Clancy. I very much appreciate that, Congresswoman, and I want to be clear about one thing. I wasn't suggesting that we would send primary care providers to camp for 3 weeks and then they would be OB-GYNs by any stretch of the imagination. This was more to serve in the coordinating role and to be able to provide some basic services, but also to make sure that people got the services that they needed in a timely fashion. And I would just say that our top consultants in women's health, urgency would be her middle name, but I will be happy to get back to you about the mammography issue specifically.

Ms. Titus. Thank you. I yield back.
The CHAIRMAN. Dr. Roe, you are recognized for 5 minutes.
Mr. Roe. I thank the chairman.
And I am certainly glad that it is not 3 weeks. It took me 4 years and then 30 years of experience to get to OB-GYN camp. So I am glad to hear that, that you can't do it in 3 weeks.

Look, we want to as a group here, and I think you hear it from both sides of the aisle, we want to be able to go from good to great. And to be able to do that, though, we have to have information that is accurate and timely. And I looked at the memo today we were sent on the RVUs, and I know this is not a big thing, but I think it is a symptom of what goes on in the VA. If you look at a law that was passed in 2002, it appears to me when you look at the evaluation that the IG did with these five medical centers in Boston, Houston, Indianapolis, Philadelphia, and looked at the staffing levels we are talking about for specialty care services, it has taken 12 years and we still don't know what they are. I mean, this law was passed in 2002, and it is 2014, and we are still talking about, well, we don't know what our staffing needs are.

Well, that is not complicated. I can tell you, having spent 30 years doing what I did, it is not hard to figure out what your staffing needs are. If you can't get somebody in to see a cardiologist, you need a cardiologist. You don't need another study or anything to figure that out.

And I don't understand, again, the accountability. When this didn't happen for 12 years, and then last week, last Friday, we found out that 80 percent of the people in senior levels at the VA got rewarded for doing a great job, and yet we completely ignored this metric, it doesn't appear that there is any penalty whatsoever for not following the law. Am I wrong? I mean, why wasn't this done?

Dr. Lynch. Congressman, I can't speak to what happened before I got here. I can speak to the fact that following the IG report the recommendations were taken seriously. We are a year ahead of time in meeting those recommendations. By the end of this year we will have productivity standards for all specialties in VA and we will be able to use those moving forward to make decisions about where we need to supplement support for physicians or to provide additional physicians.

Mr. Roe. Let me just ask a question again. Is there any accountability at all? I mean, because this 12 years went by. I mean, this information should have been available to you all where you could use it to help prevent what just happened.

So anyway, I want to also go on to a couple of other things. Mr. O'Rourke brought up, and I totally agree with this, is that really there are two issues at stake. Look, the backlog is not going to be a big deal. We can fix that one very quickly, I think. And today I got a call from Memphis, Tennessee, a physician down there put together in 3 days, with the University of Tennessee system, with the Methodist Hospital, they will see any veteran, primary care or specialty care, including oncology, in 72 hours. They can do that. Our group can do that. It can be done across the country. So the backlog is very simple to solve.

A much more difficult decision is the culture of the VA, where we go 12 years we don't follow what the law is, where we reward people at senior levels for doing I don't know what. Maybe some of them did a really good job, but others clearly did not because we see the failings right now. And let me just give you an example, a brief example.

I went to my eye doctor today right here in Washington, a retina, I have a little retina problem. The doctor said he had been trying to get to the VA here, the retina specialist, to help out. He had a patient that was supposed to see a doctor in January this year with a retina problem, at the VA. It snowed that day. The doctor couldn't get in. So they made the next appointment in June. That is this month. Well, when the retina guy finally saw him, the doctor saw him at the VA, they rushed him over to the retina specialist because the guy had a detached retina. For 5 months he didn't get treated.

We had another call today, this physician I talked to in Memphis had a fellow who took 8 months to get to an oncologist outside the VA, recommended a biopsy. That took 4 months. The man has cancer they probably can't treat now.

We cannot have a system that treats our veterans this way. And we have a system out there of private physicians who want to help. They want their veterans, like me, and Dr. Wenstrup, and others, like this young man right here. I should show you this when we get through today, Dr. Lynch. I want you to see this because they want to help. And I think they are there to help. I think their intentions are right. I think your intentions are right. I truly believe that you want to make things better for veterans.

But we do have that second one. That first one, the backlog, we can take care of that. I have no doubt in a year we can get that. Last six months we can get it fixed. That second one, though, that culture in the VA is going to be much, much harder and it is going to take a lot of work and honesty and transparency from the VA senior people to us so we can help you go from good to great.

I yield back, Mr. Chairman.

The CHAIRMAN. Thank you very much, Doctor.

Mr. Michaud.

Mr. Michaud. Thank you.

When you figure the cost as far as putting out services from the VA, do you also consider the savings; i.e., we heard from Kris Doody in charge of the ARCH program. Actually we are able to save the VA about $600,000 during that pilot program for mileage. So do you consider the cost savings as well or just the cost compared --

Dr. Lynch. I think when we look at how we manage excess demand, we need to determine whether we can provide that service more economically within the VA or whether it is better for us to buy that in the community. I think that is an important decision. We do know the community costs, we can calculate. We do have the information to determine what it would cost us to hire those physicians and to provide care in the VA. And I think if we can do it more economically, and at less cost in the community, then that would be an appropriate thing to do.

Mr. Michaud. Yeah, but considering all of the factors, I mean, it might cost X within the VA for a certain specialty care, it might seem to cost more outside for that same specialty care, but when you look at the savings with mileage reimbursement, it is most cost efficient to do it outside versus inside. So do you look at the whole cost?

Dr. Lynch. Yes, sir, I think we do, and we will.

Mr. Michaud. Okay. My second question is, of the three key elements of capacity, supply for clinical providers, amount of services providers can deliver, modern IT infrastructure, of these three, which one poses the greatest challenges to the VA?

Dr. Lynch. I would say, based on our aging infrastructure, our greatest challenges are providing the physicians adequate space to see patients and giving them the support they need to see patients efficiently. It is hard to separate. I think IT is a challenge as well, but I do think we do have an electronic medical record. It is not a perfect record. It is in the process of evolution and improvement. But I think our greatest challenges are in our support for our physicians and then the space for them to provide care in efficient fashion.

Mr. Michaud. Okay. My last question is, when you look at the wait lists, I know some facilities have an automated system where they call in, it is automated. Depending on how long it takes them to get through the menu, they might hang up. Say, the heck with that, they are not going to bother. Are they counted into that wait list, and if so, how can you track them?

Dr. Lynch. People call into the VA for a number of reasons, so it is going to be difficult to know what they are calling in for. We do measure, however, abandonment rates, and we do measure time to answer our telephone system. And we are working to improve those so that that won't be a problem.

Mr. Michaud. Thank you, Mr. Chairman.

RPTS HUMISTON

DCMN HUMKE

[9:29 p.m.]

The CHAIRMAN. Dr. Wenstrup? Mr. Takano.

Mr. Takano. I just want to follow up with a question.

The CHAIRMAN. Yes, sir.

Mr. Takano. So I am a little confused by interoperability of records. Can you help me explain maybe what Dr. Benishek was trying to tell me about there is no interoperability?

Dr. Clancy. Well, this is a case where you are both right. The second stage of the so-called meaningful use, this is the series of stepped incentives, right, that CMS has put in place incentivizing private sector providers to adopt electronic health records and the like, not just to buy the stuff, but to actually use it in such a way as to improve quality of care, that second stage of meaningful use actually requires that providers be able to share some information with other providers. So you are right that meaningful use is actually a path to getting us to a place where we can share all the information.

I think it is fair to say that many providers are finding this challenging, so Dr. Benishek is also correct when he says, give me a break, because if you are thinking about actually just uploading all information from one to another, that is actually much, much steeper and likely a bit far off, but I think your original assertion that, in fact, the incentives put in place by the High Tech Act are setting us in the right direction, and I just wanted to make the point that VHA is complying with all of those.

Mr. Takano. Well, because my understanding, having spoken to some physicians who do work at VA hospitals is that, they do appreciate the VistA medical record, and I am quoting him, the information is all there, and it seems common sense to me that if the records are integrated --

Dr. Clancy. Right.

Mr. Takano. -- that enhances the integrated care within the system, so within the VA system, doctors can --

Dr. Clancy. Absolutely.

Mr. Takano. -- pass this information around.

Dr. Clancy. Yes.

Mr. Takano. And so the concern that was raised in many hearings was the lack of interoperability with DOD and their medical record system and the billions of dollars that we have not been able to spend in a way that we have interoperability, and we listen to situations and cases where service members and veterans, their healthcare was greatly compromised.

And so I have been listening to these hearings and understanding that the challenge with being able to move into opening greater opportunities for our veterans to access non-VA care is this interoperability challenge. So that is why, you know, I was raising the question.

So it would seem to me that if we want to move more in this direction, that we are going to have to encourage private physicians and care groups to be able to communicate with the VA's record system.

Dr. Clancy. Yes. And so I think your other question or statement was that if this were written into the PC3 contracts, that the providers who had met the meaningful use requirements and so forth would get preference, or to the extent that they could contract with such providers, that would be a good thing in terms of coordinating care is a very fabulous idea, so we will take that back as well.

Mr. Takano. Thank you. I yield back.

The CHAIRMAN. Ms. Brownley. Ms. Titus. Mr. Jolly.

Mr. Jolly. Sure. Mr. Chairman, I just have a very quick follow-up.

Doctor Lynch, I want to go back to the fiscal year 2014 appropriations question I asked you for a point of clarity.

I understand you mentioned the VA's in the process of working with outside providers. Is that just a general statement or are you suggesting that the demonstration project congressionally directed in the fiscal year 2014 budget is currently being implemented?

Dr. Lynch. It is being implemented, Congressman. Can I get you the information on the sites where that is being provided at this time?

Mr. Jolly. Yeah, you certainly could. There are about six or seven of us that actually wrote a letter to the secretary on May 7th asking for an update on the implementation. I know you have got a lot of letters coming your way right now, but it is a matter of concern, because it was done with such specificity. Even the criteria were put in the congressional report as to how the centers were to be evaluated, so I just want to make sure we are talking apples and apples here, that this is fiscal year 2014 demonstration project.

Dr. Lynch. Let me work with our Office of Mental Health operations --

Mr. Jolly. That would be great.

Dr. Lynch. -- get you the information that you need and make sure we have talking apples and apples.

Mr. Jolly. Sure. And I will leave a copy of the letter. It was May 7th, there were seven of us that signed it. I will put it in your hand when we leave tonight, and I appreciate a response. Thank you very much.

Dr. Lynch. Thank you.

The CHAIRMAN. Ms. Kirkpatrick, you are recognized for 5 minutes.

Ms. Kirkpatrick. Thank you.

Dr. Lynch, I just have two questions. Is there a complaint system within the VHA, something like a hotline that a veteran can call and someone gets back to them about their complaint?

Dr. Lynch. Dr. Clancy, do you want to take that?

Dr. Clancy. Yes. Every facility has a patient advocate. And, in fact, they get complaints, they get all kinds of calls, and that is actually tracked in terms of time to resolution and so forth. That all of the patient advocates now come under an Office of Patient Center Care and Cultural Transformation.

So we have begun working with them a bit from the quality and safety side to try to figure out how could we learn more from what they are hearing, because we are noticing that a number of private sector organizations are taking to heart just how important and useful it can be to learn from the patients themselves. So --

Ms. Kirkpatrick. So is that information looked at nationally, nationwide, not just -- it doesn't just stay at the local facility?

Dr. Clancy. Yes. There is a national database.

Ms. Kirkpatrick. And my second question is, are you consulting with the VSO's on how to engage innovation in the system when it comes to scheduling these appointments?

Dr. Lynch. We have not been communicating directly with the VSO's. I think we certainly have been looking at ways that the VSO's can help us understand how the veterans are perceiving our care and the timeliness of that care. I think there is a huge opportunity there.

Ms. Kirkpatrick. I agree.

And you know, Chairman Miller, I think it might be good to have a hearing where we hear from the VSO's about their suggestions about how to fix this problem.

I yield back. Thank you so much.

The CHAIRMAN. Thank you very much, Ms. Kirkpatrick.

We do have one hearing that will be coming up in several weeks that will be specifically geared towards the VSO's, and it is at that particular hearing that we will invite the Secretary to be here to hear their recommendations as well.

Dr. Ruiz? Ms. Kuster.

Ms. Kuster. No, sir.

The CHAIRMAN. Mr. O'Rourke? Anybody -- oh, Mr. Walz, I am sorry. You are recognized for 5 minutes.

Mr. Walz. Thank you, Mr. Chairman. And again, thank you both for being here. And listening to the testimony, I appreciate it.

I have sat here almost in this exact same seat for seven and a half years and just like you with the VSO's and the VA as partners and advocates to get this right for veterans, but I am going to come back to -- and I oftentimes in those years prefaced and said that I am your staunchest supporter, but I will be your harshest critic when it needs to be.

I am going to come back to something you said, Dr. Clancy. You said, and Dr. Roe brought this up and Mr. O'Rourke, and I brought it up with several others that this is the time to think fundamental change, this is the time to think big, and I found it interesting that you focused, Dr. Clancy, on the triage, which of course needs to be done with these veterans right now, and called what we were talking about a second order question. I would argue, had you addressed that earlier, we would have never had Phoenix, we would have never had those things. So I am going to ask you, are both of you clinically credentialed?

Dr. Lynch. I am not currently -- well, not clinically credentialed at this time. I certainly have been for the last --

Mr. Walz. Can you see patients?

Dr. Lynch. I cannot see patients, no.

Mr. Walz. Dr. Clancy?

Dr. Clancy. I haven't for a number of years. I have actually looked into what would be required --

Mr. Walz. But you are both doctors?

Dr. Clancy. Yes.

Mr. Walz. And we don't have enough doctors. So I am going say what -- the Vietnam Veterans of America made this suggestion to you, and you said -- and the question was asked, you have a contract with them.

This is what they said you needed to do to fix this in Phoenix. All VHA staff with clinical credentials and training who are not currently in direct service providers need to see patients 4 days a week. Get out of the administrative office and go see patients.

If you are serious about this triage, I would think you would be turning over every stone to find a physician who is already in the system and the reason I am bringing this up, it may not seem like a fair question, but the ability to call fundamental cultural change a second order question, and we will get to it when we get this done.

Dr. Roe is right, you can multitask. Get that done. That is, of course, a priority, but not addressing this, we are going to come back here again and that is more of a statement and believe me, it pains me that we are at this point, it pains me if all the good work we do gets erased by this, but it once again confirms to me this is cultural, it is leadership, it is structural, and it runs deep.

I yield back.

The CHAIRMAN. Thank you very much, Mr. Walz.

Following up with your line of questioning, how many physicians are there in the system who don't see patients because they are in administrative roles?

Dr. Lynch. I don't know, Mr. Chairman.

The CHAIRMAN. Would you find that out for us?

Dr. Lynch. Yes, sir.

The CHAIRMAN. Thank you very much.

The CHAIRMAN. And in your testimony, you mentioned that--or in answer to a question that somebody had about how much money was being spent to help solve the backlog problem, I think the number that you used was about $312 million being made available for your access initiative, you mentioned the funds were centrally located. Can you give me an idea of where the funds were supposed to be spent?

Dr. Lynch. I will get that information for you.

The CHAIRMAN. Is the one hundred and--or $312 million part of the planned $450 million carryover that the department had already budgeted for 2015?

Dr. Lynch. I can't answer that, Mr. Chairman. I will get the information for you.

The CHAIRMAN. I can answer it.

The CHAIRMAN. It is. And I guess the big question is if almost half a billion dollars sitting there in the bank, then why do we have a backlog the size of the one we have? How did we get here?

I don't think anybody even to this day knows how the culture became so corrupt that people would falsify records, and in some cases I believe criminally, that we would cause veterans to wait months and years, that we would -- and, look, that is $500 million for carryover this year. We have had a couple of years just recently that have been a billion dollars carried over, and I don't think the public understands.

People are running around saying more money, more people, more money, more people. Five hundred million sitting there that could have solved this, and nobody within the central office or the department was blowing the whistle saying, we needed to spend that. It was almost as if they were trying to keep it for a nest egg for next year, because if you carry it over, then it goes into the base budget and we have got to fund it again, and that is how the bureaucracy grows.

So with that, thank you so much for being here. We appreciate both of you.

Members, thank you for attending. This hearing is adjourned.

[Whereupon, at 9:41 p.m., the committee was adjourned.]

APPENDIX

STATEMENT FOR THE RECORD

PARALYZED VETERANS OF AMERICA

HOUSE COMMITTEE ON VETERANS' AFFAIRS
CONCERNING EVALUATING THE CAPACITY OF THE DEPARTMETN OF
VETERANS AFFAIRS TO CARE FOR VETERAN PATIENTS
JUNE 23, 2014

Chairman Miller, Ranking Member Michaud, and members of the Committee, Paralyzed Veterans of America (PVA) would like to thank you for the opportunity to provide our views on the capacity of the Department of Veterans Affairs (VA) to care for veterans. No group of veterans understand the full scope of care provided by the VA better than PVA's members—veterans who have incurred a spinal cord injury or dysfunction. PVA members are the highest percentage of users among the veteran population, and the most vulnerable when access to health care and other challenges impact quality of care.

PVA believes that the quality of VA health care is excellent, when it is accessible. In fact, VA patient satisfaction surveys reflect that more than 85 percent of veterans receiving care directly from the VA rate that care as excellent (a number that surpasses satisfaction in the private sector). The fact is that the most common complaint from veterans who are seeking care, or who have already received care in the VA, is that access to care is not timely. PVA believes that VA's access issues result from the broad array of staff shortages within its Veterans' Health Administration (VHA), which brings into question the VA's capability to provide care to veterans when it is needed—VA's capacity. Evaluating the capacity of the VA to care for veterans will require comprehensive analysis of veterans' health care demand and utilization measured against staffing, funding, and VHA infrastructure.

Demand and Utilization

Evaluating VA's capacity to provide health care to veterans must include an accurate depiction of the demand for specific health care services. Unfortunately, it is obvious by the thousands of veterans who have been placed on wait lists for VA care that the demand for VA health care is much higher than what has been presented by the VA over the past several years. The VA has manipulated scheduling practices and uses inadequate staffing ratios to misrepresent the demand for VA health care services. For instance, a shortage of nurses within the SCI/D system of care has resulted in VA facilities restricting admissions to SCI/D centers (an issue that we believe mirrors the larger access issues that are being reported around the country). Reports of bed consolidations or closures have been received and attributed to nursing shortages.

When veterans are denied admission to SCI/D centers and beds are consolidated, leadership is not able to capture or report accurate data for the average daily census—demand. The average daily census is not only important to ensure adequate staffing to meet the medical needs of veterans; it is also a vital component to ensure that SCI/D centers receive adequate funding. Since SCI/D centers are funded based on utilization, refusing care to veterans does not accurately depict the growing needs of SCI/D veterans and stymies VA's ability to address the needs of new incoming and returning veterans.

Additionally, within the SCI/D system of care recent projections for long term care SCI/D beds are questionably low. In VISN 22 (Southern California and Southern Nevada) the VA called for 30 long term care beds per the Capital Asset Realignment for Enhanced Services (CARES) model, which estimated demand for health care services in order to determine capacity of its infrastructure to meet that demand. It seems logical to presume that more aging veterans over time will need extended care services in Southern California, not fewer. However, VA advised us that new, lowered projections based on the Enrollee Health Care Projection Model (EHCPM) dictated a decrease in scope of new construction for the San Diego SCI/D center in VISN 22. This leads to serious concerns about future timely access to specialized care. Moreover, the EHCPM fails to account for suppressed demand that can lead to false assumptions about future utilization and negatively impact hiring and staffing. Such situations severely compromise patient safety and serve as evidence for the need to enhance the nurse recruitment and retention programs to build capacity.

Evaluating VA's capacity to provide care will require the VA's commitment to transparency and the implementation of policies, procedures, and systems that will allow for the collection of data that accurately reflects the demand for VA health care in primary care and specialty care, and specialized services.

Staffing

PVA believes that the issues we are facing involving veterans' access to VA care are primarily a reflection of insufficient staffing and by extension a lack of capacity. The SCI/D system of care is one of the crown jewels of the VA health care system. Spinal cord injury care is provided using the ''hub-and-spoke'' model. This model establishes the 24 spinal cord injury centers that exist within the VA system as the hubs of care. All other major medical facilities in the system serve as outpatient clinics (spokes) that direct and refer care back to the hubs. This model has proven to be very successful in meeting the complex needs of PVA's members. In fact, this model system of care has been so successful that the VA used the same model to establish the poly-trauma system of care.

Unfortunately, the ability of the SCI/D centers to function properly is dictated by the numbers of qualified SCI/D trained staff that are employed within the system. As a result of frequent staff turnover and a general lack of education and training in outlying ''spoke'' facilities, not all SCI/D patients have the advantage of referrals, consults, and annual evaluations in an SCI/D center. This is further complicated by confusion as to where to treat spinal cord diseases, such as Multiple Sclerosis (MS) and Amyotrophic Lateral Sclerosis (ALS). Some SCI/D centers treat these patients, while others deny admission.

VHA Directive 2008–085 mandates 1,504 bedside nurses to provide nursing care for 85 percent of the available beds at the 24 SCI/D centers across the country. This nursing staff consists of registered nurses (RNs), licensed vocational/practical nurses, nursing assistants, and health technicians. Unfortunately, the SCI/D centers recruit only to the mandated minimum nurse staffing required by VHA Directive 2008–085. As of April 2014, the actual number of nursing personnel delivering bedside care was 161.9 FTEEs below the minimum nurse staffing requirement. Factoring in the actual average acuity level, there is a deficit of 746.2 FTEE between nurse staffing needed and the actual number of nurses available. The low percentage of professional RNs providing bedside care and the high acuity level of SCI/D patients put these veterans at increased risk for complications secondary to their injuries. This lack of adequate staffing can also lead to veterans being denied care or placed on wait lists, and despite their need for care, these veterans are not taken into account when VHA staffing ratios are established or the demand for care is evaluated. Thus, allowing VA to operate below capacity.

In order to monitor staffing issues and ensure they are addressed by the VA, PVA developed a memorandum of understanding with the VA more than 30 years ago that authorizes site visit teams managed by our Medical Services Department to conduct annual site visits of all VA SCI/D centers as well as spoke facilities that support the hubs. This opportunity has allowed us to work with VHA over the years to identify concerns, particularly with regards to staffing, and offer recommendations to address these concerns. Our most recent site visits have yielded the information that is included below. This information reflects the Bed and Staffing Survey as of April 2014 for beds, doctors, nurses, social workers, psychologists, and therapists in the SCI/D system of care.

Physician personnel across the SCI/D system are below the required staffing level by 21.8 FTEEs. Social workers are below the requirement by 15.2 FTEEs. Psychologists are below the required level by 15.4 FTEEs. Finally, therapists are 33.4 FTEEs below the required level. As mentioned previously, the actual number of nursing personnel delivering bedside care is 161.9 FTEEs below the minimum nurse staffing requirement. The nurse shortages alone resulted in 114.0 SCI/D beds staffed below the minimum required number. Factoring in the actual average facility acuity level, this amount increases to 372.9 SCI/D beds staffed below the requirement. This means that there are currently 281 unavailable SCI/D beds throughout the system. If this number is adjusted based on the actual average facility acuity level, this amount increases to 539.9 unavailable SCI beds throughout the system. This absurdly staggering number has proven easy to dismiss by leaders within VHA who insist that we provide by-name lists of veterans with SCI/D who languish on waiting lists rather than interrogate the merits of our claim and objectively examine their own data.

These facts are simply unacceptable. The statistics reflect the fact that many veterans who might be seeking care in the VA are unable to attain that care. We believe that these staffing shortages exist not only in the SCI/D system of care, but across the entire VHA. Therefore, we recommend that an evaluation of VA's capacity include a comprehensive analysis of VHA staffing needs to include the recently identified veterans who were denied care, or are on wait lists for primary care. We also recommend the VA conduct outreach in its specialized systems of care to identify eligible veterans in need of care and ensure they have access to the VA.

Funding

While insufficient staffing can be traced in some areas to the VHA inefficiently managing the resources it is provided, limited funding provided over many years has superseded the savings that can be generated from operational efficiencies and increased demand for health care services. The Administration (and previous Administrations) has requested wholly insufficient resources to meet the ever-growing demand for health care services. Meanwhile, the VA has also committed to operational improvements and management efficiencies that are not adequate enough to fill the gaps in funding and not realized anyway. Similarly, Congress has been equally responsible for this problem as it continues to provide insufficient funding through the appropriations process to meet the needs of veterans seeking care.

For many years, the co-authors of The Independent Budget—AMVETS, Disabled American Veterans, Paralyzed Veterans of America, and Veterans of Foreign Wars—have advocated for sufficient funding for the VA health care system, and the larger VA. In recent years, our recommendations have been largely ignored by Congress. Our recommendations are not "pie-in-the-sky" wish lists based on nothing. They reflect a thorough analysis of health care utilization in the VA and full and sufficient budget recommendations to address current and future utilization. Moreover, our recommendations are not clouded by the politics of fiscal policy. Despite the recommendations of The Independent Budget for FY 2015 (released in February 2014), the House just recently approved an appropriations bill for VA that we believe is nearly $2.0 billion short for VA health care in FY 2015 and approximately $500 million short for FY 2016.

While we understand that significant pressure continues to be placed on federal agencies to hold down spending and Congress has moved more towards fiscal restraint in recent years, the health care of veterans outweighs those priorities. Until Congress and the Administration provide sufficient resources so that adequate staffing and capacity can be established in the VA health care system, access will continue to be a problem.

VA Infrastructure

Inadequate funding for VA infrastructure has weakened the capacity of the VA to provide care to veterans. This year the Administration requested $561 million for Major Construction. This included funding for only four primary projects and secondary construction costs—this despite a backlog of construction projects that requires a minimum of $23 billion over the next 10 years in order to maintain adequate and serviceable infrastructure.

If the Administration refuses to properly address this construction funding problem, then we ask Congress to fill this void. Ultimately, if VA is not provided sufficient resources to address the critical infrastructure needs throughout the system, then it will have no choice but to seek care options in other settings, particularly the private sector. Maintaining the capacity of the VA as a comprehensive health care provider and increasing the number of veterans seeking care within the private community is fiscally impossible. Therefore, funding VA's infrastructure needs is critical to its ability to provide safe, quality health care.

VA's Capacity to Provide Care to Disabled Veterans

Within the VA health care system, the capacity to provide for the unique health care needs of severely disabled veterans—veterans with spinal cord injury/disorder, blindness, amputations, and mental illness—has not been maintained as mandated by P.L. 104–262, the "Veterans Health Care Eligibility Reform Act of 1996." This law requires VA to maintain its capacity to provide for the specialized treatment and rehabilitative needs of catastrophically disabled veterans. As a result of P.L. 104–262, the VA developed policy that required the baseline of capacity for the spinal cord injury/disorder system of care to be measured by the number of staffed beds and the number of full-time equivalent employees assigned to provide care (the basis for PVA's site visits today). This law also required the VA to provide Congress with an annual "capacity" report to ensure that the VA is operating at the mandated levels of "capacity" for health care delivery for all specialized services. Unfortunately, the requirement for the capacity report expired in 2008.

PVA's Legislation staff, in consultation with PVA's Medical Services Department, identified reinstatement of this annual "capacity" report as a legislative priority for 2014. We have also worked extensively with our partners in the VSO community, as well as with Congressional offices to formulate legislation that would reinstate the annual "capacity" report. This report affords the House and Senate Committees on Veterans' Affairs, and the veteran stakeholders, the ability to analyze the accessibility of VA specialized care for veterans in the areas such as SCI, mental health, women's health, and polytrauma. Currently, legislation is pending in the House Committee on Veterans' Affairs—H.R. 4198, the ''Appropriate Care for Disabled Veterans Act''—that would reinstate this report. We urge the Committee to consider this legislation as soon as possible. While this legislation focuses on VA specialized services, such a reporting requirement for all of VHA every few years would allow VA and Congress to have a more accurate reflection of what is needed to maintain VA's health care system.

Mr. Chairman and members of the Committee, we appreciate your commitment to ensuring that veterans receive the best health care available. We also appreciate the fact that this Committee has functioned in a generally bipartisan manner over the years. We call on this Committee, Congress as a whole, and the Administration to ensure that veterans get the absolute best health care provided when they need it through the VA. PVA's members and all veterans will not stand for anything less.

Information Required by Rule XI 2(g)(4) of the House of Representatives

Pursuant to Rule XI 2(g)(4) of the House of Representatives, the following information is provided regarding federal grants and contracts.

Fiscal Year 2013

National Council on Disability—Contract for Services—$35,000.

Fiscal Year 2012

No federal grants or contracts received.

Fiscal Year 2011

Court of Appeals for Veterans Claims, administered by the Legal Services Corporation—National Veterans Legal Services Program— $262,787.

Letter to Gibson From Michaud

June 27, 2014

The Honorable Sloan Gibson

Acting Secretary, U.S. Department of Veterans Affairs

810 Vermont Avenue, NW., Washington, DC 20420

Dear Mr. Secretary:

Committee practice permits the hearing record to remain open to permit Members to submit additional questions to the witnesses. In reference to our Full Committee hearing entitled, ''Evaluating the Capacity of the VA to Care for Veteran Patients'' that took place on June 23, 2014, I would appreciate it if you could answer the enclosed hearing questions by the close of business on August 8, 2014.

In preparing your responses to these questions, please provide your answers consecutively and single-spaced and include the full text of the question you are addressing in bold font. To facilitate the printing of the hearing record, please e-mail your response in a Word document, to Carol Murray at Carol.Murray@mail.house.gov by the close of business on August 8, 2014. If you have any questions please contact her at 202–225–9756.

Sincerely,

MICHAEL H. MICHAUD

Ranking Member, MHM:cm

Questions: From Rep. Negrete McLeod

1. One criticism of VA is that doctors do not see enough patients in a single day compared to the private sector. Former VA doctors have explained to my staff that VA does not have enough ancillary staff to allow doctors to only perform direct patient care. A physician in the private sector can come in and immediately begin addressing the patient's medical condition because other staff have already checked their vitals and completed other preparatory work. Why does VA not have as much ancillary staff as the private sector and if they need more funding, why have they not asked for it?

2. How is prioritizing appointments for veterans with service-connected disabilities?

a. Is VA tracking the population of veterans that are seeking care for service connected conditions?

b. How long they have to wait for an appointment?

Responses: From VA

HOUSE COMMITTEE ON VETERANS' AFFAIRS
FULL COMMITTEE HEARING
"EVALUATING THE CAPACITY OF THE VA TO CARE FOR
VETERAN PATIENTS"
JUNE 23, 2014

1. One criticism of VA is that doctors do not see enough patients in a single day compared to the private sector. Former VA doctors have explained to my staff that VA does not have enough ancillary staff to allow doctors to only perform direct patient care. A physician in the private sector can come in and immediately begin addressing the patient's medical condition because other staff have already checked their vitals and completed other preparatory work. Why does VA not have as much ancillary staff as the private sector and if they need more funding, why have they not asked for it?

VA Response: As the Nation's largest integrated health care delivery system, the Veterans Health Administration's (VHA) workforce challenges mirror those of the health care industry as a whole. Internal Medicine physicians, largely primary care providers, are the largest component of the Veterans Health Administration's (VHA) physician workforce. The support staff ratio for VHA primary care providers is targeted at 3 support staff per primary care provider. Similar to the private sector, VHA support staff are trained to support patient care efforts and enhance productivity of providers by performing many ancillary functions. The second largest component of our physician workforce is psychiatric physicians. The support staff ratio for psychiatric physicians is approximately 6 staff per psychiatrist. While there are no nationally accepted mental health staffing standards, VA continues to evaluate whether this represents the optimal ratio. For specialty physicians (e.g. cardiology, gastroenterology) the support staff ratios are markedly lower than that of the private sector, with VHA on average at 1.4 support staff per physician versus the external benchmarks of 3 support staff per provider. VA is working with facilities to assess staffing levels, align them with productivity demands, and address any shortfalls through the use of alternate strategies. As VA continues to refine staffing models, we will ensure our Veterans receive their care in a timely and efficient manner.

2. How is VA prioritizing appointments for veterans with service-connected disabilities?

VA Response: Regulation 38 CFR 17.49 explains that Veterans with a need for serviced-connected care or those with service-connected disabilities rated 50 percent or greater based on one or more disabilities or unemployability have priority when scheduling appointments for medical services or inpatient care.

Veterans on the Electronic Wait List for appointments are taken off by priority group. Those with service-connected disabilities rated at 100 to 50 percent are removed first; 50 to 0 percent are removed next; and then Veterans without a service connected disability.

a. Is VA tracking the population of veterans that are seeking care for service connected conditions?

VA Response: Yes. As an example, in fiscal year 2013, Veterans Health Administration treated 2,085,991 Veterans for a service- connected condition. Of our 1,451,775 Priority 1 Veterans who have a service-connected disability rating of 50 percent or more, 1,237,698 had some service-connected care. Therefore, 85 percent of Priority 1 Veterans had some service-connected care.

b. How long do they have to wait for an appointment?

VA Response: As of July 2014, the data report from the VHA Support Service Center indicates for new patients, the average wait times are as follows: Primary Care = 26 days; Specialty Care = 24 days; Mental Health = 15 days. New patient wait times are calculated using the date the appointment was created. For Established Patients, calculated from the Desired Date, the average wait times are Primary Care = 5.13 days; Specialty Care = 5.70 days; and Mental Health = 3.46 days. For additional details and updates regarding VA patient access data visit our web site; http://www.va.gov/HEALTH/docs/VAMC—Patient—Access—Data—20140731—CondensedChart.pdf